To SHOUT (Jennifer Quinton Chally)

Tackling the housing crisis

With publicly owned construction

Direct Labour Organisations

Thanks for all your support Tony O'Brien

Tony O'Brien

Preface

"Once again Tony has brought to life the daily struggle of working-class people to find a safe, secure and affordable home in Tory Britain. His lifetime as a union activist, convenor in Southwark, and leadership in the struggle for working class advancement - both at work and socially - is matched only by his political determination to win the fight for a home as a right and the necessary national programme of council house building required to achieve it. His historical, political and economic analysis of the need for such a programme to be carried out by Direct Labour employed by our councils nails the argument against the ideological privatisation of services. His case for Direct Labour to build, maintain and repair our housing stock is correct and compelling. We must value council housing as we value our NHS, it's a national asset to be proud of, we own it, it must be available to all and it's something we must fight for as hard today as we always have. 'Tackling the Housing Crisis' is more than an account of and argument for collective struggle, it is a call to action that we need to heed."

Steve Turner, Deputy General Secretary UNITE

First published in February 2018

Updated 2ND edition published October 2019

This is the second edition of my book that was first published in February 2018. It includes most of what is in the first edition but now adds 60 new pages. These new pages focus on housing, adding my close connection with Southwark Council Housing and some of the main fascinating history behind social housing, which I originally promised would be in a separate publication. I have also updated the information on construction Direct Labour Organisations (DLOs) This new book records some of the welcome changes for DLOs and council housing that are now starting to take place since they were advocated in the original publication. One year on from bringing all of Southwark's responsive housing repairs in house the council has declared its DLO a success and its support for the future.

The timing for publishing this 2nd edition coincides with unprecedented upheaval over Brexit and the prospect of a general election taking place. For us the outcome must be the election of a Labour government. This is the only way that we can begin to reverse the many years of decline we have seen in council housing and building DLOs.

Research published in September 2019, by Heriot-Watt University for the National Housing Federation had estimated:

- 8.4 million people in England are living in an unaffordable, insecure or unsuitable homes impacting all ages across every part of the country
- 3.6 million people are living in an overcrowded homes
- 2.5 million are unable to afford their rent or mortgage
- 2.5 million cannot afford to move out, living with parents, or an ex-partner
- 1.7 million are in unsuitable housing, many being older people
- 1.4 million are in poor quality homes
- 400,000 are homeless or at risk of homelessness: including those sleeping rough, living in shelters, or in temporary accommodation or sofa-surfing
- 3.6 million people could only afford to live decently if they were in social housing with rents on average 50% cheaper than from private landlords
- It said the country needed 340,000 new homes every year, including 145,000 social homes, to meet the housing demand.

Front page cover

Picture of Southwark Building Direct Labour Organisation (DLO) workers 1982 at Hyde Park, central London. After hearing from a nurse at a mass meeting in the North Peckham civic centre about reasons for their hospital workers' strikes Southwark Building DLO workers voted to have a one-day strike in their support, and a coach load took part in the national demonstration and rally in Hyde Park in London.

Back page cover

Picture of some of the Southwark Building DLO workers and myself in 2018 who attended the 1st edition book launch held at the DLOs depot at Frensham St in Southwark

Preface

Contents

Acknowledgements

Acknowledgements

This book could only have been written because of those workers in Southwark's Building DLO who have supported their unions' Joint Shop Stewards Committee over many years in its battles to enhance and defend our organisation. I have set out to record many of these stories in this book.

Our strength has also been shown in our joint actions with others – actions of co-operation and solidarity in the fight for social justice, some of which I have recorded in this book.

There are many other trade union activists in Southwark and throughout the country who have contributed to the fight for our rights, many of them are now deceased. We built on their efforts and achievements and remember that without their sacrifice our standard of living would be much worse than it is today.

I would like to thank Dot Gibson, Chis Corrigan, Bronwen Handyside and Chaz Stoll who have provided much-needed expertise in the editing and promotion of the book.

Thanks also to Neil Tasker and the shop stewards for all their support.

What is a Building Direct Labour Organisation (DLO)?

I hope those who read this book will come from different backgrounds. Those who have worked in Building Direct Labour Organisations will know what this means while others may not.

For those who don't know, here is a brief explanation:

DLOs are public-sector building works organisations.

While variations exist, all DLOs are governed by the rules and democratic accountability which exist in local government and are mostly based within a council's housing department.

Unlike private contractors who operate to make a profit (generally at a rate of 25% or above) DLOs exist to provide a quality construction service with any surplus returned to the local authority to provide more of the services that are so vitally needed.

DLO workers are directly employed by councils who deduct income tax, National Insurance and pension contributions from their pay.

Private sector contractor workers in the main are not directly employed. They obtain work through employment agencies, most of which then pass them to umbrella companies who deny workers their full entitlement to wages, holidays, sick pay, pensions, health and safety, and trade union representation.

In contrast, building workers who work for council DLOs:

• Have local and regular employment, contributing to the local economy

• Have pay and conditions that are negotiated through trade unions

• Achieve high standards of welfare and health and safety

• Benefit from high quality training and apprenticeships

• Are more accountable for the work they carry out

Who needs contractors when DLOs can do much better?

DLOs were originally set up to overcome the problems created by the system of corrupt contracting. Successful DLOs call into question the necessity of a contracting system with its anti-competitive contract-rigging, price-fixing, unsafe work practices and the victimisation and blacklisting of trade unionists.

The main difference is accountability. Residents elect councillors to Local Authorities to carry out the services they need. Trade unions and council tenants have a greater ability to influence councils if these councils employ workers directly in Building Direct Labour Organisations.

Author background

I started working in 1963, aged 15, for a shop-fitting company which did French polishing until I became an apprentice carpenter-joiner in 1964. My first-year apprentice wage was £3 a week, and-I immediately joined the trade union "Amalgamated Society of Woodworkers" (the forerunner of UCATT and now UNITE) and at the age of 19, while still an apprentice, I became a delegate to and executive member of Lambeth Trades Union Council (TUC).

I followed in my father's footsteps, who was an apprentice carpenter-joiner in 1928 at the age of 14. My dad died aged just 60 having been worn down by the building industry. I remember him recounting the very telling stories of his working conditions when he had been a young apprentice. His father had to pay an apprentice indentured fee to the company, and, he was not paid any wages. He slept in the joinery workshop.

I was always inspired by my father who, despite suffering many hardships, went on to become a trade union activist who continually fought for workers' rights.

On my first job, after finishing my apprenticeship in 1968, I became a shop steward. This was at a Greater London Council (GLC) new-build direct labour construction site in Southwark. Later, I became the union convenor on a large housing development site in Mile End, East London. This site helped to spearhead the great national building workers' strike in that area of London in 1972. I worked on over 20 small and large private construction sites becoming a steward or convenor on many until I joined Southwark council Direct Labour Organisation in 1975. Shortly after, I became a shop steward and then full-time union convenor. I held this position for the next 37 years, until I retired in 2012.

Involved with numerous trade union and progressive campaigns, I became founding secretary of the Construction Safety Campaign in 1988 and led the campaign until 2013. I have written a book on its first 22 years, published in 2010.

Using my own practical knowledge in construction safety, I studied, got a diploma and became a chartered member of the Institution of Occupational Safety and Health (IOSH).

In 2013, the Construction Safety Campaign presented me with its "Robert Tressell Award" and in 2014 my union UCATT awarded me its life-time achievement award at its national conference.

I remain a branch officer of the Southwark and Bermondsey branch of UCATT (now part of UNITE), having been its secretary for the last 40 years.

Author background

Since leaving Southwark Council I am actively involved in the Southwark Pensioner Action Group, and the National Pensioners Convention, as a member of its National and Greater London area executive committees.

Introduction

The main part of this book is about my own experiences of working in both private and public sectors of the construction industry, my fight for security of employment, decent pay and safe working conditions.

There are not many books out there concerning the struggles of building worker/trade unionists and the hostile environment we endure when we try to organise and survive. I'm sure that there are hundreds of other great stories from building workers that can be told; this is just one of them.

It is a pity that written support for DLOs is confined to short pamphlets and news items in what are mainly trade union publications. This is no surprise to me when big business controls most of the media with all its bias in favour of private sector employers. These employers, together with governments, have always worked against the need to have Direct Labour Organisations.

A national public sector DLO is the alternative to the many construction scandals that have hit the news.

The Carillion bankruptcy; Persimmon directors' £ms in bonuses; Public Finance Initiatives' £200 billion cost to the taxpayer; the deliberately inflated costs of land and housing, just to name a few. So, let's get our message across. We need a huge campaign against all that is being thrown at us, so that we can win the fight for Council Housing and council-run building Direct Labour Organisations.

Since writing the first edition of this book, many councils are now starting to set up DLOs or expand on existing building DLOs. This has followed on from the decision of the 2018 Labour Party policy conference to support building DLOs.

Foreword

By Neil Tasker (Southwark Council Unite Building Workers' Convenor)

There is a housing crisis! Homelessness is on the increase, as is poverty, with many ordinary working families now reliant on foodbanks to make it through the week. What a sad state we are in, in a so-called civilised country. The system appears to work for the few to the detriment of the many.

I hate the term 'social housing'; it implies that council housing is now only for people at the lowest ebb of society, a last-ditch resort. As a society we have regressed in respect of housing provision for ordinary working families.

Under successive governments council housing has been sold off en-masse since Thatcher's 'Right to Buy' Housing Act in 1980. This, when coupled with the dramatic decline of new-build council homes from the mid-70s to virtually zero, tells part of the story as to why we are, where we are.

What do we need? Mass building of truly affordable council housing!

Who should do it? Directly employed workers!

The construction industry is broken, and the norm is for main contractors to employ workers on their sites on exploitative 'bogus self-employed contracts', where workers are often paid through pay roll companies, with no proper sickness or holiday pay, as it is 'rolled up'.

Currently the government's Construction Industry Scheme (CIS) is the stand-alone tax scheme and enabling tool for the construction industry to uniquely classify workers as self-employed but tax them at source. This means by the nature of their engagement the vast majority are bogusly depicted as self-employed.

There is a real skills shortage and an ageing workforce which can only be addressed through a planned approach to proper trade apprenticeships, to produce the quality skilled trades men and women so desperately needed to build new homes across the country.

Council homes used to be built by DLOs and there is no reason why this still shouldn't be the case.

It's hard to see a real change until we have a progressive socialist government which has a vision that works for everybody and not just the 'Fat Cats'.

I have worked for Southwark Council as a plumber for more than 30 years, since I left school. At that time a real apprenticeship was a sought-after job.

Foreword

I went to college alongside others that were on a Youth Training Scheme (YTS), a government initiative which linked training to cheap labour.

I was one of approximately 60 apprentices recruited that year at Southwark and on day one at our induction, Tony O'Brien the building workers stewards' convener addressed us, outlining the history of trade unionism and the benefits of membership.

At Southwark we were already benefiting from the local trade unions' intervention, as we were being paid significantly more than our YTS counterparts and were all given a quality starter-set of hand tools. It was an easy choice to make and all in the room signed up to the trade union relevant to their trade.

Since the merger of UCATT with Unite in January 2017, effectively all the building trades now fall under Unite at Southwark Council with 98% of building workers being trade union members.

At the age of 21 I was elected as the plumbing shop steward at the Silwood Depot in Debnams Road; at that time the council was providing all the council's repairs from six depots across the borough. Successive governments since, have decimated not only the council housing stock but the Direct Labour Organisations (DLO) that service them as well.

It is testament to Tony and the stewards' committee, but most importantly the tenants and the workforce that, though somewhat diminished, Southwark Councils DLO still exists.

I took over the baton from Tony and was elected as the convenor steward upon his retirement in 2012. It is often said I have a very different style, but I can assure you that the sentiment is the same, and we have continued campaigning for council housing and council directly-provided services, where the tenant and not the shareholder can truly be at the centre of what we do.

In November 2014 UCATT representatives met informally with Eleanor Kelly and Peter John (CEO and Leader of Southwark Council) to discuss the future of Southwark Building Services. Ultimately the meeting was about our future and what was required to realise our aspiration of once again providing the repairs and maintenance work directly for all council residents across the borough.

Since that meeting UCATT, now Unite, have continued to 'bang the drum' and try to show what the future could look like with Southwark Council delivering all the repairs with its own (DLO).

Foreword

Following a series of strategy meetings involving both councillors and senior council officers, Unite was delighted to hear that senior council officers responsible for housing and the in-house repairs service jointly recommended to the council that from October 2018 all internal repairs across Southwark's housing stock be directly provided by Southwark's own DLO

Though this was good news, there is so much more that local authorities can do now to ensure the ethical employment of workers across their contracts by simply incorporating key requirements into their procurement processes.

Unite has developed a national 'Unite Construction Charter' which places many positive requirements on contractors tendering for local authority work. The key requirement though is to exclude contractors that engage bogus self-employed workers and insist that all staff on their sites are employed on a PAYE basis.

Jeremy Corbyn's leadership of the Labour Party has been a revelation and there is a political shift with regards to housing, with council housing high on the agenda. The need to build council homes is clear and, under a Labour government, there is now a commitment to do just that! **NT**

Private Sector of Construction Industry

Starting out working in private construction sector

I had direct experience of how Southwark council's new homes were built from 1967 to 1975. After I had completed my apprenticeship. I worked on many of their new-built projects which were mostly carried out by private sector contractors. As a Southwark resident I was very happy to travel the short distances to get to work, when before I had travelled many hours each day before even starting work. The Southwark building sites I worked on included: Lorrimore Road Square, North Peckham, Camden, Gloucester Grove, Bonamy, Heygate, Acorn and the Aylesbury Estates. All these estates other than Lorrimore Square have now been demolished, Aylesbury is partly demolished and facing the threat of further demolition. The corrupt activities which resulted in these estates being built as well as their early demolition, I regard as vandalism and a criminal act against construction workers and the people of Southwark.

The above picture is of a protest held against the employment of 'lump labour' (companies which used workers to avoid tax and deny them their employment rights). It was at a site where a contractor had been building new homes for Southwark Council in the Camberwell Green area of South East London in 1974.

18

Starting out working in private construction sector

Jack Kennedy, the UCATT regional organiser can be seen on the left side of the picture speaking to the workers. Fourth from left, next to the man with the black tie can be seen the late Fred Stansbury who was Southwark DLO convenor from 1969 to 1975, from whom I took over from in 1975. Also, in this picture were Southwark DLO workers: Denis Smith, John Potter and Harry Evans. Others included well-known trades union activists: Pat McGowan, Vic Heath, Bill Skelly, Ollie Manning, and George O'Driscoll (1)

The first job I had after coming out of my apprentice training was at flats being built for the construction branch of the Greater London Council (GLC) at Lorrimore Square in Walworth. I quickly followed in the footsteps of my father by becoming the carpenters' shop steward on this job. I wrote off to get my shop steward's credentials from my union, then known as the Amalgamated Society of Woodworkers (ASW). Within a few days the regional organiser for the ASW 'Jack Kennedy', came onto the site and asked for me.

Jack knew my father as a trade union activist, and he came from the same South London Irish Community. Jack greeted me, asking how my Dad and the family were. He then said, to my complete surprise: "Why in God's name would you as a young lad (I was then only 20 years of age) want to become a steward?"

I was a bit shocked but undeterred by his remarks, and after a few words he came to accept that I was determined to become a shop steward for the workers on this site. It was only later after a few years of experience I would discover that becoming a trades union activist meant you would suffer discrimination. I then understood that Jack Kennedy's remarks were out of concern for me, because of the persecution I would have to face. I soon discovered how difficult it was having to survive in a construction industry that had very brutal employers.

After Jack's visit I received my shop steward's credentials as the representative for the carpenters on this site, and within a few weeks I achieved several improvements in working conditions. In those years asbestos was rife on construction sites, with very little information over its dangers being available. Most information over asbestos was put out from the employers and asbestos manufacturers who claimed it was safe to work with. It was only my Dad who had made me more aware of its dangers. So, when I raised my concerns to management over working with asbestos, they became annoyed and especially when I insisted, I be supplied with a dust mask.

Starting out working in private construction sector

They also did not like the extra time that was involved when I refused to cut up asbestos inside sparsely ventilated bathrooms and kitchens where it was being installed.

I was also involved in installing huge fire-check doors to the entrances of underground garages. These doors were solid and weighed a ton, being nearly 3 inches thick, seven feet high, 3 feet wide and lined with asbestos. Again, I refused to carry out this work in a confined place and without a dust mask. I insisted on having the support of a labourer to help me carry and manoeuvre these doors. Someone had to make a stand and besides it was hard to get support from other union members without first taking the lead.

There was one lesson you learned very quickly if you became a trade union activist in the construction industry. If you were lucky enough to get a start on a job and survive, then some time, sooner or later, you were likely to be transferred to jobs that involved long distances to get to, and that's exactly what management proposed for me. The second lesson I learned was, however hard it was to achieve, you always had to try and bring workers with you if you were forced to take a stand against management. Easier said than done, as on this job I found getting support from my fellow carpenters for my stand over these issues was very difficult. Most of them had far longer service with the GLC and they expected those with less service, like me, to be the first to be transferred. I was fortunate in that there were many other construction sites in Southwark, so I refused the transfer because I'd rather work locally than having to face travelling two to four hours a day even before starting work.

I went to my union branch meeting to make a complaint about being forced to travel long distances or be sacked. I then found the union had a National Joint Agreement with the employers which included the employers' right to transfer workers to any jobs they had. The only concession that came with this agreement was workers could claim a travel allowance that was called the 'Building Workers Travel Allowance' (BWTA). But this did not make up for the huge disadvantage building workers and their families suffered due to managements' use of the agreement to get rid of so many trade union activists.

I later got a start working for 'Wates' on the Camden Estate council housing contract in Peckham Road. I was surprised when I got to work on this job for several weeks without being asked for my National Insurance number (the National Insurance number was known to be used as the identifier to blacklist workers).

Starting out working in private construction sector

Finally, they asked me for it and the following day I was sacked. This all made sense when two years later I read in the local "South London Press" that the timekeeper was found guilty of pocketing wages from making fraudulent claims for the numbers of workers employed on this site.

It seemed that with all his excitement from the money he pocketed on behalf of invisible building workers he must have forgotten to ask me for my National Insurance number.

I also worked on Southwark Council's DLO new-build division on their North Peckham Estate site. This work was being carried out under an arrangement with Bovis. The agreement with this company meant that they would be the senior management for the council's direct labour new-build division and in return they would be paid a set fee.

All work was carried out by sub-contractors other than that of labourers, carpenters and bricklayers who were directly employed by the Council. By then, I had quickly learned to keep my head down, knowing I would be sacked if I raised any trade union concerns without first trying to establish support for trade union organisation on the job. After a few weeks, I was given a schedule of productivity targets with rates that included doing second-fix asbestos-lined panelling around pipe work to bathroom flats.

I dreaded this as I would again have to raise my safety concerns with management about the dangers involved in carrying out this work, and then face being labelled as a 'troublemaker' for doing so. I knew, because there was no active trade union organisation yet established on site that could protect me from victimisation, my days on this site would be numbered if I raised my concerns. So, I was surprised when the foreman told me he wasn't concerned about my hesitation to do this work as he had other carpenters who were quite happy to do so, especially when the payment for the productivity targets were quite attractive. I only hoped that these workers would heed my warnings to protect themselves from the dangers involved.

I was then put on work in the underground garages which involved establishing concrete upstands that made individual car bay areas. The productivity price for doing this work was dreadful. I found out that other carpenters were increasingly complaining about the productivity prices being too low for them to be able to establish any reasonable pay. I then decided this was the best time to act and got the word around to the carpenters I felt could be trusted that we should get together after work in a pub across the road to discuss the matter.

Starting out working in private construction sector

Unfortunately, within an hour of me doing so management must have found out by having a spy among one of the carpenters - as I was immediately sacked.

They gave me the excuse that I was not producing enough shuttering work. The real reason was a fear of having any trade union organisation on the job.

This was so evident when I was told to stop work immediately and was literally chased across the site when I unsuccessfully tried to find the whereabouts of a Mr. BH. Who I was told was the union convenor. Unfortunately for me management got their way. Sacking me on the spot had the effect of frightening most of these carpenters from meeting me later in the pub.

I worked on the Gloucester Road Gleeson site building new flats for Southwark. I quickly found that there was no trade union organisation and again decided to keep my head down until I could build up some support. This was the first job I worked on which had a factory type method of constructing large concrete sections on site. These pre- formed concrete structures would then be lifted by crane and despatched to various parts of the site. I was put to work with a gang of carpenters, steel fixers and labourers on producing these huge concrete sections.

The work was located close to the main site's gates. One day, I'd seen Jack Kennedy, the Amalgamated Society of Woodworkers (ASW) union organiser walk through the main gate towards the site offices. About an hour later when Jack came out of these offices, he recognised me and came up to me to express his anger about not getting any co-operation from management in planning with them to have trade union subscriptions deducted from workers' pay. While Jack was talking to me, I could see two site foremen looking at us. I was not too happy with this when my previous experiences taught me that, without first getting support from workers on the job, I could be singled out for discrimination because of my association with a union. It would have been better had Jack contacted me outside the site to see how best we could work together to get the job organised. The fact was that the main priority of all construction union organisers was to get trades union subscription from workers, leaving little time for them to work with trades union activists to see how best they could be protected from any of management's attacks.

So yet again, I was told I was laid-off. This time the reason given was due to workflow, as the pre-cast concrete work was being halted until other work on site was completed. I was frustrated when the union office did not get back to me after I complained about what had happened, but after a few days I got a start on another job.

Starting out working in private construction sector

In 1968, I worked on the Aylesbury Estate site. This was a huge project built for Southwark Council by 'construction company John Laing' and was to become Europe's largest council housing estate. There were numerous disputes on site when I was there. Two of the main ones were over tea breaks and toilet facilities. Suddenly management had decided to close the site canteen from being used for tea breaks. They felt the time taken for having tea breaks was too long.

This they said was because of the time taken to get to and from the canteen. Yes, this building site was huge, at least half a mile in length. Management, however, never felt responsible for supplying canteens at various distances at the site to alleviate this problem. The workers on the site were not going to have any of it. When tea break time came around, they simply walked to the canteen, sat down in protest and got their sandwiches and flasks out to have their break. Laing, also for the same reasons, instructed workers not to use the site's toilets. Instead, they supplied buckets at various points on the tower blocks that were being built. Again, workers refused to comply and eventually management were forced to back down.

It is important that history is revisited on what are human rights issues for the working class. Issues around tea break strikes are nothing new. It was in 1946 that Hugh D'Arcy who later would become a leader within UCATT, was one of those who led the wave of tea break strikes that were held on many construction sites in Edinburgh, Scotland. This was later followed by actions of workers elsewhere that forced the employers to backdown on their attempts to do away with tea breaks.

Even in the 1960-70s, it was never easy to get workers to take on the job of shop steward because of the naked intimidation from construction companies. This was also the position on the Aylesbury Estate job when the sole carpenter shop steward, an old Jamaican socialist named Ron Fairclough told me he was receiving all sorts of intimidating threats from various subcontractors on the site. Because of his age, he was not happy facing up to the physical threats and asked me if I could take over from him as the carpenters' shop steward. He had asked that a UCATT organiser hold a meeting of the 100 carpenters on the site. I felt sorry for Ron, so I agreed to put myself forward, while at the same time being a bit reluctant as I was a bit battle weary from other union activities on my previous jobs.

There was a good turn-out at the meeting, despite Laing management's insistence that it had to be held in the dinner break.

Starting out working in private construction sector

As soon as the UCATT organiser Jack Kennedy started the meeting there was an almighty crash followed by a brick that was about 18 inches away from hitting me on the head where I was sitting at a canteen table.

The meeting was abandoned as pandemonium followed with workers running about trying to discover who was behind this attack.

Surprise, surprise, or should I say no surprise when a few days later Laing's management transferred both Ron and me, with me being transferred to a job in Sutton.

It was then that Laing finally got rid of me when they sacked me from the Royal Marsden Hospital extension site in Sutton.

This occurred after a short time on the job, when severe cold weather conditions meant the trains from Peckham to Sutton were irregular and severely delayed due to frozen rail tracks. But no tolerance was shown to me for my genuine reasons for being late for work. They did not hesitate in using this as an opportunity to sack me.

It's this kind of method that is used to get rid of so many good trade union activists: transferring workers to distant places and isolating us. So, when it comes down to it, the real reason for my sacking, and then the blacklisting, was that myself along with many other workers refused to shit in buckets in the open. We refused to not have proper tea breaks that should be held in a canteen provided for that purpose and finally I was finished for being a few minutes late for work due to trains not running on time because of severe weather and subsequent frozen rail lines, but of course, the real reason was for being a trade-union member.

In 1969, I worked on a refurbishment job at the Russell Hotel at Russell Square in central London. This job was being carried out by a company named Trollope and Colls. While initially given hardwood second fixing, (second fixing is work done after the main structure named as first fixing is carried out-for example the framework) which I was good at. I was taken off this work to do what is called shuttering work that involved constructing supports for the renewal of the external concrete balcony floors. This didn't make much use of my joinery skills and after I complained, it wasn't too long before I was transferred to another refurbishment job. I later found out that Trollope was being paid a guaranteed fixed day rate for each worker they supplied on the Russell Hotel job, so they were not too pleased with the likes of me who was a threat to the large number of workers they falsely claimed for, when I insisted on having work.

Starting out working in private construction sector

After that I was transferred to another Trollope and Colls job just on the other side of Russell Square at the British Museum. I was put to work mainly carrying out second fixing works in the new printing rooms.

I was again transferred in 1971 to William Willetts-a subsidiary of Trollope and Coles. This was a large site with several hundred flats being built for Tower Hamlets council.

After a month, I got elected as shop steward and soon after got two other stewards elected, then I became the building trades union convenor on this site for the then newly merged "Union of Construction Allied Trades and Technicians" - UCATT.

UCATT was formed in 1971 from mergers of my union the Amalgamated Society of Woodworkers with two other main construction trade unions the Amalgamated Society of Painters & Decorators and the Amalgamated Union of Building Trades Workers, as well as the much smaller Association of Building Technicians.

The driving force for these mergers was the need to get to grips with the emergence of "labour-only contracting" and its worst form, the "LUMP" that had started to develop in the early 1960s. Since then, this had grown into various forms of forced self-employment and casual working. This cheated workers of proper pay and conditions and created non-unionised workforces. Trade union rank and file activists knew the only way the decline could be stopped was to campaign against the miserable low rates of pay. Activists put this into action by winning a majority for strike action at the union's conferences.

The 1972 Building workers' strike

In 1972, shortly after its formation, UCATT together with the General Municipal Workers Union (GMWU) and the Transport and General Workers Union (TGWU), who were involved in construction and civil engineering, started what was the single most important building trades unions strike in their history. For the first time ever in the building industry workers all over the country went on a national strike to demand a minimum wage of £30 for a 35-hour week and abolition of the "lump." This strike affected most major sites, effectively forcing employers to negotiate.

The background to the 1972 strike was the building boom of the 1960-70s. This was a time when there were numerous sub-contractors with many crafts making for a constantly changing workforce, differing contracts and pay rates.

Starting out working in private construction sector

Employers were constantly seeking to break union organisation by bringing in non-union labour and by blacklisting or victimising trade union activists. It was a time of labour-only subcontracting, or the "lump".

Lump workers were self-employed and thus not entitled to holiday pay, national insurance or PAYE tax deductions, instead receiving a fixed "lump" sum, supposed to cover all expenses. It was also a time between 1951 and 1971 when the building unions had lost up to 30 per cent of their members.

In April 1970, 288 delegates from 50 union branches and a similar number of stewards from sites met in Manchester and founded the "Building Workers' Charter" (BWC) as a rank and file movement. And just before the strike in April 1972, 865 delegates attended its conference.

The Charter was responsible for the unions adopting a militant claim for £30 for 35 hours. (2)

The strikes began between May and June 1972 with selective strikes on what were high-status sites - mainly hotel and larger construction jobs. It was hoped that stoppages of work on the employers' highly lucrative jobs would force them to negotiate. The national trade union leadership tried hard to keep the dispute to one of selective strikes. If this strategy had prevailed, it would have fragmented the strike and could have led to a defeat. Activists knew that this selective strike action would not be enough to secure their demands.

In a meeting of building workers in Conway Hall in Central London the demand went up for an all-out strike. My site was already out on strike and following the Conway Hall meeting many other sites in London stopped work. At the same time, other similar actions took place throughout the country. The system of flying pickets was widely developed to bring most sites out on strike. In east London, hundreds of us would meet at 6am every morning in what was then the TGWU Dockers' offices in the East End of London. We briefly discussed our targets and then got into vehicles to spread the strike.

So, what began was a very effective use of 'flying picketing' throughout the country. With only a small number of exceptions it was not at all difficult to get a clear majority of building workers to join the strike. Workers were so fed up with low rates of pay that they readily welcomed us. In those days, you did not have the security on sites you have today. So, in most cases it was quite easy to walk onto the site and call a site meeting. After explaining the reason for strike action there was no problem in getting a vote from the workers to join the strike. Following our success in getting all-out strike action the employers began to buckle and after 13 weeks agreement was reached with our unions.

Starting out working in private construction sector

The deal made never met our demands for an immediate 35 hour working week for a £30 basic rate of pay, and an end to the use of labour only and the lump.

Protests from the rank and file were massive; 12,000 building workers marched in Liverpool, demanding no settlement short of the full claim. In London, several thousand lobbied the pay negotiations.

We demanded nothing short of the full claim and that any agreement made be put to a vote of union members, yet the UCATT General Secretary Sir George Smith refused. On Tuesday 14th September 1972, the union side in the negotiations agreed a settlement with the employers.

This was despite the strength of feeling from striking building workers that the strike should be continued until the full claim was met. The union executive's control of negotiations meant that in the end this magnificent strike was sold short as they settled and called the strike off.

Nevertheless, some individual local employers had already, during the strike, agreed to pay the £30 a week claim. It was, however, despite our union leadership's actions, still a major historic victory. Our morale was hugely lifted knowing that after so many years of low pay and bad working conditions we could successfully take on our country's building employers with strike action and beat them. The outcome of the strike was a pay settlement that gave us the biggest pay rise ever. The settlement was for an immediate £6 per week pay rise for craft workers and £5 for labourers. The weekly basic, along with a guaranteed minimum bonus was raised by a further £6 and £5 respectively over the next two years, lifting the craft rate from £20 to £32 and the labourers from £17.50p to £27.20p. That was a 33% increase in pay. (3)

The aftermath from the strike was a lack of preparation by the union leadership to face the inevitable backlash from the employers, when a wave of victimisations took place, most notoriously of the Shrewsbury 24. The union leadership had succumbed to the witch-hunting of the television and press and refused to support them. Instead they should have called on all building workers to resume an all-out strike until these workers were released from prison.

The campaign to overturn the convictions of the Shrewsbury building workers won a significant victory when on 30 April 2019, halfway through a Judicial Review hearing in the Birmingham Criminal Cases Review Commission conceded the case, when It agreed to reconsider the referral of the convictions of the pickets to the Court of Appeal.

Starting out working in private construction sector

Above shows UCATT members protesting during the 1972 Building Workers' Strike (4)

The years 1972 and 1973 were a very exciting time on the Mile End William Willets site as it was for most building workers. Bolstered by the victory of the national strike, we went back to work and immediately demanded that our increased basic rates of pay be added to our productivity calculation rates. Fearful that we would take further strike action management immediately conceded.

Later the first flats began to become available for decorations after the main trades work had been completed. It was now the turn for painters to do their work. But the painters were in no mood to accept the bad pay and working conditions they were used to before the national strike. Painters tended to be paid a lot less than most other trades, yet the hard work involved was no less. They also suffered from the frequent use of arms and shoulders that gave them repetitive strain injuries. The fumes from paints and the dusts from rubbing down surfaces would have life threatening repercussions for many.

Most main contractors did not directly employ painters. Instead, they had various painting sub-contractors compete to do their work.

Because painting work was carried out towards the end of a site's work the money allocated by the main contractor would be tight. At the same time the painting contractor would be eagerly watching his balance sheet to ensure he could maximise the profits.

Starting out working in private construction sector

But the painters that came onto our site were encouraged by seeing the strength of our trade union organisation and wanted to make sure that they would gain decent pay. They immediately elected Harry Hardy as their steward. We were fortunate to have Harry as he was an experienced trade union activist.

The painters decided they wanted parity of pay with all the other main trades on the site. They knew they weren't going to get this without a struggle. Harry met with me and the other stewards to discuss the best way forward. We agreed that the painters would stop work and place picket lines on the gates, but the aim would not be to stop the other trades from going to work but to stop materials and any other painter sub-contractors going in to do their work.

On our part we would ensure nothing was done inside the site to undermine their dispute and would collect a levy from our members to pay the painters what would be the equivalent of a weekly wage while they were on strike. The strike lasted just two weeks, when the employers caved into our demands. This shows, when we are united and work closely together, we can take effective action for equality between the trades - action not just to protest but to win a victory without any major loss of pay.

Nationally, the backlash from the employers came within less than a year of the winning of the national building strike. A conspiracy began to take shape led by what was then the "Economic League" (the forerunners of the blacklisting "Consultative Association") and supported by most of the major construction companies. Evidence for that conspiracy was later found on thousands of pages in the files of 3,200 blacklisted building workers when the government's "Information Commission raided the offices of the "Consultative Association" in 2009. The highest point of that conspiracy was the taking to court and jailing of what was known as the Shrewsbury 24. Hundreds if not thousands of those names discovered on the blacklist files were involved in the 1972 building workers' national strike and what occurred after this strike.

In my case, within nine months of the ending of the building workers' national strike two workers brought on to the site at Mile End tried to physically assault me with hammers.

I was only saved from being attacked by these two thugs after I escaped from them and ran into the protection of other workers in the site canteen.

The two workers declined to follow me into the canteen and rapidly disappeared from the site. As there were no witnesses to the actual attack, management refused to make any enquiry.

Starting out working in private construction sector

Instead, shortly afterwards, they gave me notice of dismissal for refusing their request that I stop taking time off to carry out my convenor's duties.

A carpenter had warned me that he had overhead the foreman speaking to other carpenters to frighten them by saying: "should they support me they may not find further work with the company and this job was soon to be finished."

Despite this attempt to split the workforce they voted to take strike action over my sacking. The strike had limited potential for success, since most of the work on the site was coming to an end. Many workers were already transferred to other jobs or had left to find other work. Two out of the three stewards did not have any previous experience of the union, became very annoyed at the lack of any follow up action by the union, and despite my pleas they resigned as stewards shortly before the end of the strike.

Above: I can be seen in the foreground on the picket line during the strike against my sacking when I was convenor at the William Willett site in east London's Mile End. (5)

This was about 9 months after the end of the national building workers' strike. What happened to me must have happened to many others, as there always comes a crunch time for every trade union activist who has been successful in establishing and maintaining trade union organisation on their sites. It comes towards the end of the job. That's when nine times out of ten you will become excess to requirements with any old excuse being used to sack you or make you redundant and given a week or a week and a half's pay for every year of service.

Starting out working in private construction sector

Or in many cases you are sacked without any redundancy pay and told to work your notice. While any of this can happen to all building workers, it would happen more often if you had become a successful trade union steward.

After being sacked from William Willett, I had my third attempt to work with Laing, but I was recognised by a site foreman from my previous work on the Aylesbury estate. Yet again, I was sacked, after only two days on this job at Tottenham Court Road in central London.

I had-had enough and decided to 'phone the union. UCATT said they would get back to me. I decided I would wait in the site canteen until then. Management did not like me still on site talking to other workers about what had happened to me. To my delight, the picture of me being physically lifted out of my seat in the canteen and dumped outside the gate by two heavies was too much for the workers on this site to stand by and do nothing. With the help of a known trade union activist who was already on this site, Brian Craze, this then led to the threat of strike action. The UCATT organiser Pat McGowan then appeared, met management, and I was reinstated back on the job.

Above is a picture of the march from Wigan to London, in support of the Shrewsbury building workers, arriving in London.

Starting out working in the private construction sector

I was delegated to represent this Laing's site on the march from Wigan to London in support of the jailed Shrewsbury building workers and was nearly sacked for doing so but instead got a written warning. (6)

This site gave me my longest spell of employment in the private sector - nearly two years of continuous work. During this time, we had many disputes and we won most of them. We also did much to support other workers in struggle.

The picture above shows a protest in 1974 held outside the offices of the TUC prior to the sentencing of the Shrewsbury Building Workers. (7)

On the right-hand side in the background of this picture can be seen the John Laing's building site which I had worked on at Tottenham Court Road. The picture shows some known construction activists in the London area who were demanding the TUC oppose the jailing of the Shrewsbury pickets: from the left Peter Cavanagh, third from left Len Murray TUC General Secretary, then George O'Driscoll, then Billy Butler near the middle is myself and in front of me on my right-hand side holding a paper is Gary Davis and centre-right is Geoff Coleman.

Starting out working in the private construction sector

If you work in the private sector of construction, it is very rare that you would be permanently employed. So, when I left Laing's I was surprised to get an immediate start with the Housing Works Division Direct Labour Organisation of Southwark council.

What happens in the private sector affects DLOs

The fight for workers' rights in the construction private sector has a direct impact on those who work in Council run DLOs, the crucial factor being the strength of trade union organisation at site level.

In the 1970s in the private sector there were numerous individual strikes over pay and attempts to sack trade union activists. Some were successfully settled at site level. However, on the many occasions when an employer would not budge, they were taken to what was known as a "disputes panel". This consisted of the regional secretaries of the trade union federation and the building employers' federation. Often what proceeded these panel hearings was pressure on the union offices from lobbies of site workers on strike.

It was always preferable to win any dispute at site level, but when this was not possible, especially when the employer had broken national joint agreements, you could succeed in forcing a favourable outcome from the disputes panel.

Council DLOs were also boosted by trade union activists who came from the private sector to start work in DLOs.

However, today because of the government's sustained attacks on the rights of workers, the forcing of workers into bogus self-employment (over 50% of workers being self-employed) these disputes panels hardly operate and don't pay any attention to the huge amount of abuse that takes place against workers.

The same goes for council run DLOs when local authority employers have continued to try to undermine and do away with the construction unions' national agreements contained within the "red book agreement". They would have found this virtually impossible had they tried in the 1970s when DLOs employed 238,000 workers, while today they only employ a few thousand.

That's why our fight for directly employed labour in both the public and private sector of construction is so important. It's no exaggeration to say that the building industry employers have a deep sense of insecurity, hence their devising all sorts of methods to make sure they maintain absolute control at the workplace. This is not surprising when the 1972 strike showed that building workers could bring most sites in the UK to a standstill to secure the biggest pay increase in their history.

What happens in the private sector affects DLOs

Ever since then, the employers. aided and abetted by Tory anti-union laws and employment reforms (which Labour governments refused to repeal) have made sure this does not happen again. Their method of control is to deny us any form of job security.

Workers have been increasingly driven to compete against each other through the operation of different rates of pay and divisive bonus schemes.

In the 1970s and 1980s McAlpine would display bonus earnings of gangs on notice boards. Some companies such as John Laing would separate those workers who they said were established from those who they said were non-established. Wates had a grading system based on how many stars workers achieved and would display this on notice boards.

Even now the construction industry continues the system of using numerous sub-contractors with different terms and conditions of employment, rather than having all workers directly employed by the main contractor. All this divides workers and is used to prevent them from uniting around the fight for equal terms and conditions of employment.

It was a widespread practice to transfer or sack workers when their job on a site ended. There were many struggles when employers often tried to rob workers of their dismissal notice pay or statutory redundancy pay. (30)

Private sector construction workers must have workers' rights

Having an accountable and properly regulated private construction sector which complies with workers' full protection rights is good for workers in both the private and public-sector. We both gain. Private sector construction workers gain by being directly employed, having proper pay and conditions of employment, strict safety standards, apprentice training, and quality work standards. Public-sector DLO building workers gain because this would show the true costs associated with tenders submitted by the contractor companies for public sector work. This would enable DLOs to win more work when competing against contractors.

DLOs could then expand and give private sector workers the chance of working for DLOs. These workers would have the security of final salary pension schemes, full pay for absence due to injury and ill health, longer-term employment and other trade union negotiated agreements -all of which they rarely have now.

What happens in the private sector affects DLOs

Construction workers must put up a fight

The fact is, nothing comes without a fight. So, despite all the difficulties that both public and private sectors workers have, they must be prepared to come together and fight to achieve the benefits we deserve.

Private sector workers need to ask themselves whether they will continue to put up with being engaged by agencies who use umbrella companies to rip them off in their pay and allow bosses to stop them from creating what should be 100% trade union organisation on all sites; are they prepared to elect and then defend shop steward representatives from attacks?

We all know that the ability for workers to organise and best protect themselves from employer's' abuse has for a long time been greatly diminished and continues to be so because of black-listing. So, I put the question: are you prepared to make a commitment that you will stop the job every time the bosses try to refuse employment to a trade union activist? If you are prepared to do so: WE WILL WIN.

This is also a political issue – one that requires changes in employment law. Employers continue to get away with back-listing and victimising workers as the law does not protect us. It exists to protect employers. It does so by allowing them to refuse to re-employ workers who have won a wrongful dismissal case at Industrial Tribunals. If this is not stopped then nothing will change.

Trade union members will continue to be victimised and added to a growing number of those who are already blacklisted. We cannot allow this vicious practice to continue. Construction workers must get politically active. We don't want to hear any more excuses from politician as to why laws cannot be changed to protect us.

Private sector workers' employment status

We must put an end to the way so many construction workers are employed in the private sector. There is no doubt in my mind that the employers and the politicians conspire together to ensure maximum exploitation of construction workers. We have an industry that chooses to subcontract their work several times. Many workers employed by subcontractors are then required to operate via a mixture of false self-employment that is used by agencies who then subcontract their payroll to umbrella companies.

What happens in the private sector affects DLOs

By not employing workers themselves, these main contractors and sub-contractors avoid having to pay the employers National Insurance Contributions, and often don't have to pay other benefits such as holiday pay, sick pay and pensions. This false self-employment has gone on for many years. It occurs when a worker is categorised as self-employed for taxation purposes but has all the employment characteristics of an employee.

The current main method of false self-employment is through the Construction Industry Scheme (CIS), a standalone taxation scheme. Under this scheme workers are taxed at source and can make expense claims at the end of the year. Having self-employed status means workers can be dismissed without warning, even if they have worked for the same employer for many years.

Ironically the problem of umbrella companies comes from the decision by the previous coalition government in April 2014 when it cynically lied about cracking down on the false self-employment of workers engaged via employment agencies. The government said these workers couldn't be self-employed and had to be directly employed.

However, rather than put them onto PAYE and direct employment status, employers have been allowed to move these workers onto umbrella companies. Under the umbrella company system, the worker is hired by an agency at a set rate, but the sum agreed is not what the worker receives. Officially they only earn the minimum wage (although for construction workers, wages are usually boosted by mechanisms described as Performance Related Pay).

The amount the worker had negotiated goes to the umbrella company. The umbrella company levies a weekly charge for paying the worker, which can be up to £30 a week. The real crime begins as the worker must pay both the employers' and employee's National Insurance contributions. With income tax, it means that workers can lose up to 45% of their eligible earnings through deductions. On top of this, holiday pay is also rolled up into the rate, and paid weekly. When holidays are taken, they are effectively unpaid. If a worker is auto enrolled into a pension, they must pay both their own contributions and the employers.

Following all these deductions, the pay the worker expects is severely eroded. Given all the different deductions and massaging of the pay you will be unsurprised that workers genuinely do not understand their payslips.

What happens in the private sector affects DLOs

Because these umbrella companies don't recognise the collective agreements made between the Unions and the building employers through the Construction Industry Joint Council (CIJC) workers are denied many other benefits. For example, when a journey to work is longer than 15 kilometres, travel expenses must be paid, in addition to the agreed pay rate. Future pensions are also affected when they are based on basic minimum hourly rate contributions and when zero-hour contracts mean some don't even have minimum hours of work. Many of these umbrella companies are also based overseas in order to avoid liability for tax on their own profits.

UCATT (now UNITE) has produced the following recommendations

- Employment agencies and other employers should be obliged by law to employ workers directly, not via umbrella companies

- The hourly rate agreed between a worker and an employer, including an employment agency, should be the rate that the worker is paid

- There should be a legal duty on employers to make payment arrangements transparent and easy for workers to understand

- It should be obligatory for employers to pay reimbursement of travel and other expenses in addition to a worker's hourly rate

- Holiday pay should never be 'rolled up' into a worker's weekly pay

- All forms of false self-employment should be abolished, including the Construction Industry Scheme (8)

UCATT had accused the construction industry of "blatant tax dodging", calculating that for a £700 per week construction worker, Her Majesty's Revenue and Customs (HMRC) picks up more than £200 in tax when they are directly employed, but less than £159 when they go through an umbrella company. The union was behind a motion that was overwhelmingly passed at the 2016 TUC conference to fight against the use of umbrella companies. (9) (46)

What happens in the private sector affects DLOs

Above is a picture of a picket line protest of the use of 'Lump labour' at the offices of the Inland Revenue at Somerset House in London in 1973.

Following a freedom of information request in July 2017 which revealed an enormous increase in bogus-self-employment, UNITE called for root and branch reforms of employment rights. This was after new figures showed that at least 1.076 million construction workers were paid via the Construction Industry Scheme (CIS), an eight per cent increase on the figure of 12 months previously when 992,973 were paid via CIS. In total 47% of the entire construction workforce is now paid via CIS. (64)

Companies need to be shamed by demonstrations and through the media. The long-term solution requires radical reform of the taxation system and employment rights. All forms of false self-employment and umbrella companies should be outlawed, and the CIS scheme scrapped.

What happens in the private sector affects DLOs

There must be a reform of employment status laws to create only two categories of workers, employees and genuinely self-employed.

The casual nature of the industry and the lack of fixed establishments mean other reforms are also urgently needed. For example, workers cannot claim for unfair dismissal unless they are in post for two years. For many building workers a three-month engagement is a long period and two years is a lifetime.

Without these basic protection's workers are totally exposed to a hire and fire culture. Therefore, we need legislation for full employment rights from day one which must include the end of an employer's right to refuse to reinstate workers who are wrongfully dismissed.

Other reforms must include a complete reversal on the restriction of workers from taking industrial action. This right must be enabled for all workers in the UK. It's no exaggeration to say workers in the private sector are systematically being robbed due to governments which have allowed the employers to dictate the status of workers. Public sector Direct Labour Organisations must be expanded in addition to a national public construction DLO being established.

History behind the corrupt practice of contract rigging

Contractors have always formed monopoly rings to keep prices up and select those among themselves who should get jobs. Scandals involving private contractors were rife at the end of the nineteenth century particularly over public building works In London. The exposure of the corruption of the Metropolitan Board of Works, the forerunner of the London County Council (LCC), caused much public concern at the time.

Large amounts of money could be made from corrupt deals between politicians and building contractors, e.g. T Dan Smith who was a leading Labour councillor in the north east of England and John Poulson a leading architect. The extent of their corrupt practices during the 1960s was exposed and Poulson was convicted of fraud on 11 February 1974; he was jailed for five years. Smith was charged with bribery in January 1970 and in October 1973 he was again arrested on corruption charges. Evidence showed he had received £156,000 over seven years; he pleaded guilty in 1974 and was sentenced to six years' imprisonment.

Three MPs were involved but there was a legal loophole which exempted them from being prosecuted. The Poulson scandals did much to force the House of Commons to initiate a Register of Members' Interests.

History behind the corrupt practice of contract rigging

In 1968, There was a boycott by construction companies who refused to tender for work on what was then the Labour-controlled London Borough of Wandsworth.

In September 1982, Southwark Council's Public Services Committee revealed that ready-mixed concrete suppliers effectively went on strike when the council tightened up on its requirements for its one-year contracts. (10)

These contractors had ganged up on the council by refusing to submit tenders. Instead they produced their own jointly agreed contract, which they required Southwark to accept. Southwark was then forced to try and negotiate a three-month extension to their contracts.

1990 was the year in which Southwark DLO had lost a large amount of their repairs and maintenance work in the council's Bermondsey and Rotherhithe area. A company named Beazer won a 12-month contract for this work (Beazer later became part of Kier Ltd).

The actual outturn of Beazer average price for a maintenance repair was proven to be 33% higher than the same work carried out by the council's own Building DLO. This was revealed at a Southwark council committee.

In December 2006, the "Daily Mail", not known for supporting campaigns to defend public services published a statement from the head of the Local Government Association, Lord Bruce-Lockhart, which showed how private contractors were ripping off local authorities. (11)

Construction firms in the UK were fined by the Office of Fair Trading (OFT) for illegal bid-rigging in September 2009. The Governments OFT imposed fines totalling £129.5 million on 103 construction firms in England which it found had colluded with competitors on building contracts.

This decision followed an Office of Fair Trading (OFT) Statement of Objections in April 2008 following one of its largest Competition Act investigations. The OFT concluded that the firms were engaged in illegal anti-competitive bid-rigging activities on 199 tenders from 2000 to 2006, mostly in the form of "cover pricing". Cover pricing is where one or more bidders in a tender process obtain an artificially high price from a competitor. Such cover bids submitted as genuine bids, give misleading impression to clients as to the real extent of competition. This distorts the tender process and makes it less likely that other potentially cheaper firms are invited to tender. The OFT found six instances where successful bidders had paid an agreed sum of money to the unsuccessful bidder (known as a "compensation payment").

History behind the corrupt practice of contract rigging

These payments of between £2,500 and £60,000 were facilitated by the raising of false invoices. The OFT announced that its evidence of "bid-rigging" by construction companies in some 4,000 tenders involving 1,000 companies had to focus on the companies and instances where evidence was strongest. Instead of using their considerable powers to bring these companies to justice, they carried out a fast track approach by offering discount fines for companies prepared to cooperate.

Despite the scale of the bid-rigging, the OFT cautioned local authorities against banning offenders from future work, as they said that cover pricing was "widespread in the construction industry".

The OFT has the power to fine companies up to 10% of their annual turnover. More than half the companies managed to reduce the size of their fine by admitting their guilt. As a result, more than 100 British construction firms escaped with fines averaging 1.14% of their global annual turnover. One lawyer acting for several of the companies investigated by the OFT said: "For my clients, it's a result."

The OFT warned the revelation could be just the tip of the iceberg, with the practice of cover pricing described as "widespread and endemic. "Several major companies including Balfour Beatty, Carillion, and Kier were among those listed by the OFT. The United Kingdom Contractors Group (UKCG) director, Stephen Radcliffe, said: "Everybody knows, including the OFT, that cover pricing was widespread in the industry in the past".

What construction trades union activists have known over many years about fraud carried out by employers in the private sector was then publicly confirmed. That is why for us the fight for the public ownership of the construction industry is a truly important issue. Until 1998 bid-rigging was rarely prosecuted and since 1998 it is hardly mentioned. The Office of Fair-Trading task was made much easier because of the introduction of the Competition Act 1998 and Article 81 of the EU Treaty which outlawed bid-rigging. Construction employers try to excuse and cover up their corrupt practice by calling it "cover-pricing" when in fact what they are involved in is price-fixing.

We must not allow the employers to use the UK's vote in June 2016 to come out of the EU to delete the anti-bid-rigging requirements contained within Article 81 of the Competition Act 1998.

The table below lists the 103 parties and sets out the fines imposed, after all discounts including for leniency. Some fines apply to two or more companies that were part of the same infringing activity.

History behind the corrupt practice of contract-rigging

It is worth noting that many of these corrupt contractors listed below have been involved in tendering for construction work against Southwark Council's Building DLO as well as many other DLOs throughout the country. This resulted in many DLOs losing work and workers being made redundant.

Those on the list:

- H Willis & Sons £120,018.

JH Hallam (Contracts) (45% leniency) £359,588.

- ARG (Mansfield) (40% leniency) £12,128.
- J J & A R Jackson £28,963.
- Ackroyd & Abbott £49,581.
- J. J. McGinley £732,901.
- Adam Eastwood & Sons (40% leniency) £2,006.
- John Cawley (65% leniency) £5,476.
- Admiral Construction Ltd and A C Holdings Ltd (45% leniency) £17,406.
- John Sisk & Son £6,191,627.
- Allen build and Bullock Construction £3,547,931.
- Kier Regional together with its ultimate parent company Kier Group plc £17,894,438.
- Apollo Property Services Group £2,150,536.
- Lemmeleg Ltd together with its ultimate parent company Rok plc £1,387.
- Arthur M Griffiths & Sons (35% leniency) £203,592.
- Lindum Construction Co £496,017.
- B & A Construction (Leicester) £18,224.
- Linford Group £359,714.
- Baggaley & Jenkins £144,153.
- Loach Construction & Development (40% leniency) £46,923.
- Balfour Beatty Construction and Mansell plc (50% leniency) £5,197,004.
- Lotus Construction £791,062.

History behind the corrupt practice of contract rigging

- Ballast Nedam N.V. £8,333,116.
- Milward Construction (Belper) £68,766.
- Beaufort Construction £83,703.
- Morgan Ashurst plc (45% leniency) £286,593.
- Bodill & Sons (Contractors) (50% leniency) £54,848.
- North Midland Construction plc £1,543,813.
- Bowmer & Kirkland £7,574,736.
- P D H Developments £1,289.
- Bramall Construction and Keepmoat Ltd (40% leniency) £455,235.
- P. Casey & Co £287,197.
- C J. Ellmore & Company £295,979.
- P. Waller Ltd (40% leniency) £56,889.
- Caddick Construction £391,323.
- Pearce Construction £5,188,846.
- Carillion JM (45% leniency) £5,375,689 and Clegg Construction (45% leniency) £359,967.
- Peter Baines Ltd £31,119.
- Connaught Partnerships £5,568,868.
- Phoenix Contracts (Leicester) (40% leniency) £91,053.
- Crown Point Maintenance Group£3,571.
- Propencity Group (50% leniency) £98,042.
- Davlyn Construction (35% leniency) £72,916.
- Quarmby Construction Company £881,749.
- Derwent Valley Construction Ltd together with Chevin Holdings Ltd (45% leniency) £24,517.
- R Durtnell & Sons £711,115.
- Dukeries Building Company £99,773 Concentra Ltd £6,720,551.
- R. G. Carter Ltd £2,981,580.
- Concentra and Durkan Holdings £3,283,884.
- Richardson Projects Ltd £595,747.

History behind the corrupt practice of contract-rigging

- E. Manton Ltd £226,096.
- Robert Woodhead Ltd £411,595.
- E. Taylor & Sons (Southwell) Ltd £59,261.
- Robinson & Sawdon Ltd £172,661.
- F. Parkinson Ltd £174,110.
- Shaylor Construction £318,580.
- Francis Construction £530,238.
- Simons Construction Ltd (40% leniency) £838,685.
- Frudd Construction Ltd (40% leniency) £65,872.
- Sol Construction Ltd (45% leniency) £1,835,702.
- GAJ Construction Ltd £109,683.
- Speller-Metcalfe Malvern Ltd £389,758.
- G Carter Construction Ltd £91,466.
- Stainforth Construction Ltd £156,737.
- G. F. Tomlinson Building Ltd £1,269,270.
- Strata Construction Ltd (formerly trading as Weaver) (45% leniency) £692,285.
- G. & J. Seddon Ltd £1,516,646.
- T. & C. Williams (Builders) Ltd (40% leniency) £87,966.
- GMI Construction Group plc £1,752,584
- T. Denman & Sons (Melton Mowbray) Ltd £90,521.
- Geo Houlton & Sons Ltd £265,492.
- Thomas Fish & Sons Ltd (40% leniency) £170,131.
- Greswolde Construction Ltd £168,559.
- Thomas Long & Sons Ltd together with its ultimate parent company Radford Holdings Ltd £210,095.
- Hall Construction Group Ltd £269,634.
- Thomas Vale Construction plc (50% leniency) £1,020,473.
- Harlow & Milner Ltd (45% leniency) £23,170.
- Thorndyke Ltd £173,560.

History behind the corrupt practice of contract rigging

- Harold Adkin & Sons (Sutton-In-Ashfield) Ltd £5,936.
- Try Accord Ltd and Galliford Try Construction Ltd £8,333,329.
- Hay Mills (Contractors) Ltd £781,440.
- W. R. Bloodworth & Sons Ltd (35% leniency) £10,854.
- Henry Boot Construction (UK) (45% leniency) £1,074,441.
- Liggett Bros & Co Ltd £15,923.
- Herbert Baggaley Construction (45% leniency) £198,043.
- Wildgoose Construction Ltd (50% leniency) £309,204.
- Hill Bros. (Nottingham) Ltd £5,808.
- William Sapotes and Sons Ltd £342,601.
- Hobson & Porter Ltd (45% leniency) £574,507.
- William Woodsend Ltd £53,970.
- Holroyd Construction Ltd £200,784.
- Willmott Dixon Construction £4,534,760.
- Interclass Public Limited Company £464,406.
- Wright (Hull) Ltd £529,923.
- Interserve Project Services Ltd £11,634,750.
- Wager Construction Co Ltd £67,877.
- Irwin's Ltd and Jack Lunn (45% leniency) £314,933.
- York House Construction Ltd (45% leniency) £239,525.
- J. Harper & Sons (Leominster) £713.

(List of OFT bid-rigging fines; BD online; 22 September 2009) (12)

The London Builders' Conference

Below are extracts from the House of Commons debate on 7 November 1952: *Mr Percy Wells (MP for Faversham) said of The London Builders' Conference:*

"In this innocent-sounding title there exists an organisation which exercises a control over building tenders that not only makes a farce of competitive tendering but extracts large sums of money from those for whom the work is performed, without performing any service whatever to the building owner.

"The activities of this organisation are not, as the name implies, confined to London only; they are nation-wide.

History behind the corrupt practice of contract rigging

There were regional conferences up and down the country and these operate in conjunction with the London Builders' Conference. The brain behind these conferences belongs to a high grade ex-civil servant who was reputed to receive a salary on a par with that of the Prime Minister of the time.

"The scam worked by every co-operating non-member or member, as soon as he has decided to tender for a job, must immediately inform the conference chairman of his intention so to do.

"The reason for this became clear as this information was then circulated to those firms who were about to tender for the work. This allowed tenderers to know exactly with whom they are competing, and it also enables them to get together and fix upon a minimum price for this contract.

"This obligation to report was contained within the London Builders' Conference constitution and rules, paragraph 15: "should extend to all building or civil engineering work anywhere in the United Kingdom estimated to cost more than £2,500. Members must also report information coming to their knowledge about the competition of non-members.

"The next and fundamental obligation of members and their co-operating non-members to the Conference is, and here is a quote again from paragraph 18 of the Conference constitution, 'to report in confidence to the chairman the preliminary price at which he would propose to tender'. It must be noted that this information is forwarded to the Chairman of the London Builders' Conference or the regional conference, whichever it may be, before any tender has been sent to the person for whom the work is to be done.

"What happens to these prices when they reach the offices of the Conference? Are they checked by a body of experts? Not at all. The highest one-third when more than five tenders are received and the highest more than three when five or less tenders are received are eliminated. This has been described in many quarters as a racket. To what extent it has increased the cost of building it is not possible to tell, but the sum must be tremendous. It is an impudent and unjust extraction for which the owner receives no benefit."

The MP added: "That the activities of the London Builders' Conference are open to condemnation is agreed by the Royal Institute of British Architects, the Chartered Surveyors' Institute and that very reputable trade journal, 'The Builder'. A letter to over 500 members of the London Builders' Conference, dated 21st July 1952, sent out by Sir Alfred Hurst states,

History behind the corrupt practice of contract rigging

"'Because of a semi-official discussion I had with leading officers of the Ministry of Works, that Department has in no case insisted on the signature of the Declaration and no firm has been penalised on that account. I have already received from the Minister of Works the assurance, which I accept unreservedly, that this statement is not correct.'

"I mention it now to show the lengths to which the Chairman of the London Builders' Conference is prepared to go in order and I quote from the concluding paragraph of the letter to which I have referred to continue the solid front that has hitherto proved so successful. So successful in what? The fleecing of building owners." Extract from:

hansard.parliament.uk/commons/1952-11-07/debates/9a8f004b-3540-4b1b-874d-cdd99c0bfd1c/LondonBuildersConference (13)

The Builders' Conference still exists

Their website states the following: "The Builders' Conference is an independent, not-for-profit trade association providing members and the construction industry with up to the minute sales leads, market intelligence, statistical data and networking opportunities.

Established for over 80 years, we have one of the most extensive and trusted on-line databases of projects, clients, consultants and contractors in the UK. We handle over 11,000 contract opportunities each year worth more than £50 billion. Our members monitor, apply for and win work every day using our live database." (14)

There is an alternative to the monopoly of contractors and all the possibilities of contract rigging and the collusion of price-fixing deals between them. This alternative is local Council run building DLOs which can be used to measure the true value of contracts and prevent future practises of contractor's corruption.

Crimes against work of building workers and the environment

The waste of workers' hard labour and the huge damage done to our environment must be greater in the construction industry than any other activity. Let me illustrate what is happening throughout the whole country by using the practice of Southwark council house building.

Crimes against work of building workers and the Environment

In the space of only 30 to 50 years' wholesale demolition of much of Southwark Council Housing has already been carried out or is in the process of being carried out. Most of these properties were built by Southwark in the 1960s and 1970s.

Can you imagine the scale of destruction, the thousands of tons of wasted construction materials, the various plant, machinery, the use of cranes, tools and transportation? The waste of our money must add up today to tens of billions of pounds.

We tend to forget the abuse carried out towards the health of workers. Building workers carry out repetitive and physically strenuous activities, resulting in injuries, deaths, disabilities and ill-health (death and injury rates were much higher than they are today). Wasted human labour, and wasted materials and, it is we who end up having to pay for it all.

Between 1968-1974, I worked on many of Southwark Council's new build construction sites. Most have now been demolished. Huge numbers of houses which have never been replaced as social rented council housing.

I worked for Wates on the Camden Estate council-housing contract in Peckham Road and, as well as the scam collecting pay packets for "ghost workers" carried out by the timekeeper, others included extensive changes to work already done. I became aware of this after I had completed several shuttering jobs, when gangs of labourers would start to demolish the concrete structures which resulted from my shuttering work.

When I protested, asking why they were destroying my work, I was told: "There's nothing wrong with the work, it was just because the site surveyor has changed his mind." This council estate was built in the early 1970s and demolished in the late 1990s. That's less than 30 years of use.

I went on to work on building the "North Peckham Estate". This was at the time the second largest construction site in the Southwark area. Bovis ran this site under an agreement with Southwark that meant it would manage its Direct Labour New-Build division. Asbestos was in wide use with much of it used to insulate the pipework in bathrooms and kitchens. I have no doubt the hundreds of workers that worked on this site would have been contaminated by asbestos. This council estate was built between 1969 and 1975 and was demolished in early 2000s; that's just over 30 years of use.

Crimes against work of building workers and the Environment

Also, in the 1970s, I worked on the Gloucester Grove new build site, which was being carried out by the contractor Gleeson, building new flats for Southwark Council. This was a very badly designed site with interconnecting corridors that were subject to much rubbish dumping and vandalism. Most of this estate was demolished in the early 2000s – that is only just over 30 years' use.

In January 1991, Raymond Assahoun died while trying to escape from the fumes caused by a fire at Gloucester Grove Estate. The following investigations found that the large number of layers of flammable paint on the ceilings and walls of lengthy corridors, together with a wind tunnel effect, allowed this fire to spread rapidly.

This council estate was built between the late 1960s and early 1970s with most of it being demolished in early 2000s, that is only just over 30 years of use.

I worked on the Aylesbury Estate in the late 1960s for John Laing. Incredibly I found I was to be put to work on one of three large so-called "snagging gangs" of carpenters. These gangs would go around to what were supposed to be finished flats, carrying huge sheets of listed work that already been done by sub-contractors but now was required to be put right.

I found this highly unusual, as normally the provisions in contracts allowed for any faulty work to be redone within a specified timescale by the contractors who had carried out the work in the first place and without any additional payment made. Was this another scam?

Much of the fault for the bad construction of these flats was with their bad design. Internal walls were made of three-3-inch breeze block. When we came to fix the door frames and doors there was not enough strength to withstand the movement of the heavy fire check doors within them. Also, the wooden floors were uneven and moved under pressure. This was because of the meagre five-eighths-of-an-inch thick floorboards that were fixed to three-inch joists, under which were hot water pipes. The weakness of the wooden flooring combined with the heat from these pipes and the lack of ventilation caused severe twisting and warping to these floors.

Again, asbestos was used in the back panelling in the bathrooms. Cancer from asbestos was not the only danger I faced. I was given a job to erect shuttering up stands to ventilation ducts that came through each flat and then onto the flat roof on the Wendover block of flats. I found getting additional help from a labourer was nearly always impossible. It was common practice for management to deliberately discourage the use of labourers by having the labourers' time booked against the productivity rates you were paid to do the job.

Crimes against work of building workers and the environment

To do this job I was supplied with heavy eight feet by four feet sheets of three-quarter inch ply. I can remember a gust of wind taking hold of this ply when I was carrying it over the roof of the Wendover, and I had the frightening experience of being shifted close to edge, with no edge protection to stop me being blown off. I had no choice but to let go the sheet of ply. Luckily, a near disaster was averted when the ply lodged against a heavy transformer I was using and was prevented from going over the top of the roof.

Construction started on the Aylesbury, one of the largest estates in Europe, in the mid-1960s and was completed in the mid-1970s.

It still exists and has lasted longer than many others because of the tenants' ongoing resistance to its demolition and privatisation. While demolition was halted by leaseholder's successful court action, demolition has now restarted. This estate has had only 50 to 60 years of use by its tenants.

While not a Southwark Council estate. I feel my experience of the wasted use of workers' time while I worked on the Russell Hotel, Russell Square in central London is well worth a mention. This refurbishment job was carried out by a company called Trollope and Coles, and heavily funded by public money.

This hotel was only one of many hundreds which were either being built or upgraded to meet the demands of the thousands of oversea visitors expected to participate in the events surrounding Prince Charles' inauguration as the Prince of Wales in July 1969. The government had forecast there would be a severe shortage of accommodation to allow for the foreign visitors. To encourage the building companies to meet this demand, on what was a short timescale, the government offered to pay out a large subsidy for every building tradesperson used by the building employers to carry out this work.

When I applied for work on this site, I had no problem in getting a start. I was looking forward to doing the work in these hotel rooms, the period architectural features, the use of hardwoods, the moulding, the panelling work, and the joints involved were the type of work I had carried out in the joinery workshop and sites during my apprentice training.

My first job was to establish oak skirtings in one of the rooms. I was about to complete this in less than half a day when the carpenter foreman popped into the room to look at my work. He was quite happy with the quality but said, to my amazement, that "I was working too fast". I had never been told this before. I then thought he must have been a trade union-minded person to make such a remark. I asked him if I could have more skirting boards so that I could carry on completing the work in the other rooms on that floor of the hotel.

Crimes against work of building workers and the Environment

He told me to take my time in sanding down the finished work to the room and he would see me the following day.

On the following day, by the time it was 10 am I was fed up with waiting around and decided to go in search for him. I found him in the canteen and again asked him for more work. He told me that the work on the hotel was well ahead of schedule, so I would have to wait until he came to see me before I could do any more work. Rather than get bored stiff I had sharpened up my tools several times., and then decided to walk around this large hotel.

I discovered that it was teeming with lots of others who were also having to hang around to wait for work. I had many embarrassing encounters upon my walks.

One such was when I walked into one of the bathrooms to discover one of labourers making full use of it. It sounds like the scene from the film "Riff Raff" by Ken Loach, but it's true.

After speaking to other workers on the job I soon found out the real reasons why site management were quite happy for workers on this site to do less work. This was because of the Government subsidy to contractors for every single building worker they got to do this type of work. The employers weren't interested in the productive output of their workers, because they could make far more money by just cramming workers onto the job and making it last. The loss of building workers' time and the cost to the taxpayers for this work (and I suspect many hundreds of other such jobs) would have been hard to calculate, but it must have been enormous.

Because of my complaints about lack of work, it was not long before I was transferred to another Trollope & Colls refurbishment job, just on the other side of Russell Square at the British Museum.

Council Run Direct Labour Organisations

History of building Direct Labour Organisations

The London County Council (LCC) set up the first Direct Labour Department in 1882. Others soon followed. A look at the history of Direct Labour shows that many of the issues then are still the same today.

Local government's response to the failures of private contractors to provide an adequate building service led them to consider setting up their own building services as the contractors' need for profit clashed with the objectives of local government. As today, contractors formed monopoly rings to keep prices up, skimped on work and exploited their workers to keep costs down. Scandals involving private contractors were rife at the end of the nineteenth century, particularly over public building works In London. The exposure of the corruption in the Metropolitan Board of Works, the forerunner of the LCC, caused much public concern at the time. Contractors profited from such corruption, but others had to foot the bill.

The liberal bourgeoisie of London formed an alliance with the new leaders of the Labour movement in a grouping called the "Progressives" on the LCC. The Progressives were determined to ensure that such practices would not continue under the new LCC. It was this alliance that eventually led to the setting up of direct labour departments. (15)

Many factors created this alliance. In the early 1890s labour organisation in trade unions was strong. Following the success of the 1889 dock strike, new unions were emerging as unskilled workers organised alongside the traditional craft unions of the skilled workers. They demanded union wage rates on work done for local authorities and supported the demand for local authority Direct Labour. Building unions were particularly strong. Trade union membership was rising, and branches were established in areas previously little affected by trade unionism. Building trade unions were opposing the imposition of excessive hours and unfair wages by contractors.

Unemployment was high during the depression years up to 1895 and the Government's attempt to mollify rising discontent through public relief works was proving no real solution. Local authority Direct labour was seen by many as a more effective way of creating employment.

Building work, particularly in London, was one area in which employment could expand. There was much work to be done in the construction of housing, public buildings and the developing suburbs.

History of building Direct Labour Organisations

There was a rapidly changing political position within the LCC with the emergence of a Labour Group including such figures as John Burns, Ben Tillett and HR Taylor of the Operative Bricklayers Society. They saw municipal services as being a direct challenge to the failures of capitalism.

An alliance was forged between the Progressives, who wanted to increase the efficiency of capitalism, and Labour leaders who wanted socialism: both groups sought to expand the provision of municipal service, in part through Direct Labour.

The Progressives gained control of the LCC in 1889, defeating the 'Moderates' who represented the interests of contractors. One of their first acts was to bring in a clause enforcing trade union conditions and pay on all contracts given out by the council. Contractors retaliated by putting in outrageous tenders. it was against this background and to destroy the monopolistic position of contractors that the growing demand for a Works Department was accepted in 1892. Its first work was the building of York Road sewer in Battersea. The lowest estimate received for this when put out for tender was £11,000. The new Direct Works Department completed the work for £6,854.

The lead given by the LCC in setting up their Works Department was soon followed by Battersea in 1894 and West Ham in 1896. Their work was varied, from the building of a power station In Battersea to the LCC's contract for all school furniture. Some of the first council estates were completed by Direct Labour. Battersea undertook all its own building work. The departments were equipped with many workshops, and the LCC even owned its own brickworks.

The Moderates who formed the main opposition group to the Progressives did their best to hamper the activities of the new DLO. They dressed up their real intentions when in the name of "municipal reform" they claimed that direct labour was costly and took away local employment. When they subsequently gained control of the council, they ruthlessly proceeded to destroy the Works Department and sacked 3,000 workers. So, began the repeated threats to direct labour made by private contractors, anxious to survive their own crises by seeking public sector work.

After 1918, particularly in the north, the number of DLOs steadily rose. From 1919-1920, with growing unrest over housing conditions, 70 new departments were set up. Direct labour was the only way to get housing built in the face of excessive tenders by private contractors.

As in the 1890s. This upsurge of DLOs reflected strong labour organisation.

History of building Direct Labour Organisations

Alongside negotiations on wages and conditions which were taking place at the national level through the National Association of Building Trades Councils (the forerunner of the National Federation of Building Trades Operatives) (NFBTU), discussion also took place on the question of post-war reconstruction, future housing needs, and the role to be played by the building trade unions in the post-war years. It was in this context that DLOs were being established. Local authorities were initially encouraged in this activity by the Government following successful direct labour experiments in both Newbury and Liverpool.

Between 1919-1920. 70 new Direct labour schemes were sanctioned, these were in: Barnes, Basingstoke, Bedford, Birmingham, Cadworth, Itchen, Kingston-on-Hull, Lancaster, Ledbury, Liverpool, Llantrisant, Manchester, Norwich, Swansea, Tonbridge, Tottenham, Walsall, West Hartlepool, Worcester. (16)

Both working conditions and wages in the departments were better than those in the private sector, including a 44-hour week and payment for "wet time" (i.e. when work is disrupted due to bad weather conditions). Many DLOs played an active part in their local authorities, sitting on joint committees with councillors.

Despite the setback from the slump years in 1920-1924 DLOs continued to build a growing number of council houses. This was so successful that by 1927, with the onset of a drastic slump in house building the employers' organisation, the National Federation of Building Trades Employers (NFBTE), launched an attack in a pamphlet entitled: "The Menace of Direct Labour". The Labour Research Department responded with a book on direct labour which pointed to its importance to the Labour Movement. (17)

Bermondsey Borough Council in the 1930s was, amongst others, one of the earliest councils in London to have its own directly employed building workers. Bermondsey Borough Council built the Spa Road Estate, Ironically, when so many of the council housing properties have been pulled down, the Spa Road Estate is still standing nearly a century after it was built.

The council was one of the more progressive in the 1920-1930s when you compared the conditions of work with those of other workers at the time. Bermondsey had a pioneering socialist MP, Doctor Alfred Salter and his wife Ada Salter.

Ada did much pioneering work to improve the conditions for workers in Bermondsey this included research work on social housing, seeking not only to demolish the slums but to put in their place model council houses.

Building workers employed with Bermondsey Council were given a whole number of paid allowances. They got paid in periods of bad weather and were even allowed paid time for feeding and looking after council horses used to transport plant and materials to construction sites. (18)

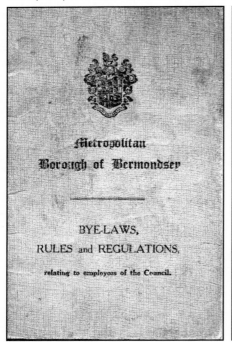
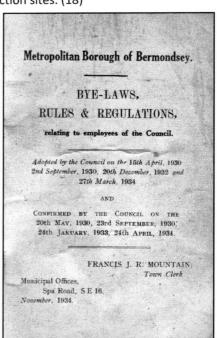

Seen above are the front and inside pages of the rules that applied at the time.

The emergence of many DLOs after the First World War was repeated after the Second World War. As in the immediate post First World War years, this was a period of strength and militancy in the building trade unions. As building prices soared, local authorities needed a method which both checked the prices quoted by contractors and got the work done.

By 1948, Local authority house building reached an unprecedented height of 175,213 dwellings and many local authorities set up their own DLOs as an expedient to cope with the new housing requirements. At the same time, many formerly disbanded DLOs were reconstituted.

The LCC, for example, re-established its DLO in 1951 following an experimental scheme started in 1948. Alongside this support for DLOs, the unions were also demanding nationalisation of the industry.

History of building Direct Labour Organisations

By 1949 the number of DLOs had doubled compared with 1939, coinciding with the emergence of new Labour Party strongholds and the renewed Government commitment for large-scale council house building programmes.

Soon after the return of the Tories to power in 1951, came a fall in the numbers and standards of Local Authority housing. But private industry now enjoyed boom conditions, and private contractors could draw labour away from DLOs. They had no pay restraints to comply with, whereas local authorities were empowered to pay only the lowest local level trade union rates, with bonus schemes limited to 20% of basic earnings. The effective operation of DLOs was consequently hampered by a shortage of labour. Political restrictions on direct labour were once again disguised in the form of economic necessity. Private contractors had nothing to fear from direct labour during most of the 1950s, and hence no reason to mount substantial campaigns against it, although periodic criticisms persisted.

Many DLOs in the 1950s and 1960s, including Southwark's old Camberwell Borough Council had operated what was a metal tag system (as on the Docks) for workers to report for work. I know this as my father worked for the old Camberwell Borough Council for several years in the 1960s. He was then engaged daily and was given a metal tag when reporting for work in the morning and had to hand it in at the end of the day.

In 1959, the Government suddenly imposed the recommendation that new build work carried out by direct labour meant winning every third contract in competition with local and national firms. It comes as no surprise that the construction industry had just gone through one of its periodic recessions. Total output had risen rapidly since 1951 but fell in real terms by almost a fifth between 1957 and 1958.

Despite these conditions the number of operatives employed in DLOs grew from 70,000 in 1955 to 122,000 in 1964. Another obstacle to their expansion was the growing use of and encouragement in the 1950s and 1960s of industrialised systems, not often employed in DLOs.

Many authorities were either too small and therefore lacked the resources to break away from traditional techniques or were unable to build up enough plant because of repeated closure threats.

Industrialised construction was the use of 'heavy prefabrication' mainly used in wall panels in reinforced concrete, which were mass-produced in factories. It was claimed at the time that industrialised buildings could be erected faster with a less specialised workforce, increasing financial benefits.

History of building Direct Labour Organisations

However, this has not turned out to be true as older more traditional brick-designed buildings have lasted longer, have been less hazardous. For example, the Ronan Point Tower block collapse in East London.

The Labour Government in 1965 revoked the 1959 restrictive rules that DLOs must be able to win one in three contracts. This was now left at the discretion of the local authorities. Then direct labour was encouraged "to play a full part in the house-building programme." Although, as we have seen, their economic position limited the role they could play, DLOs reached their peak size in 1967, employing 200,000 workers.

Lambeth DLO workers protest the Lump and the rundown of their DLO in 1978.

History of building Direct Labour Organisations

Above can be seen Camden DLO workers in 1976 in a day of action against the Lump (19)

The attacks on DLOs continued when for example the new build side of Birmingham Direct Works, was closed by the Tories in 1969, and its plant sold off. This was to give more work to private contractors in the area, who were once again experiencing a down-turn in output, particularly for public sector work.

Contractors argued that DLOs should act in competition, and, as a result, a new Ministry circular was put out insisting that DLOs "compete for a considerable and representative proportion by value of work". But during the boom years of the early 1970s private contractors were less interested in local authority work. Councils had difficulty getting contractors to undertake work and had to pay exorbitant prices. Only the building programmes of those councils which had promoted powerful DLOS were largely unaffected.

Private companies had widely used the system of lump labour to avoid tax, deny workers employment rights and to discourage workers from being organised in trades unions. This system continues today with the same aims but in a different form.

From the end of the nineteenth century, DLOs were at the forefront of constructing and maintaining Britain's social housing until their decline with privatisations that took place mainly after 1980.

History of building Direct Labour Organisations

The DLOs exemplary training programmes for apprentices were also a casualty of this political shift, one of the major contributory factors for the crisis in the supply of skilled labour for the entire UK construction industry.

Between 1945 and 1969, local authorities built, owned and let over 4 million dwellings, amounting to 59% of total housing construction. Most local authorities maintained their own DLOs largely tasked with repair and maintenance of existing housing stock but also building new housing, in some cases on a large scale. These include, for example:

- Glasgow Corporation's DLO, Glasgow City Builders, which built 63% of the city's post-war housing.
- Greater London Council DLO, which in 1978 employed 5,000 workers, had a turnover of £73m and carried out 90% of the maintenance of its 205,000 dwellings,
- Manchester DLO, which over a 15-year period had by 1976 built 17,500 dwellings, 56 schools and 17 other major buildings, employing 5,500 building workers.

Local authorities were not the only employers of direct labour. Other public bodies, such as central government and what were previously nationalised industries, had similar building workforces. Even some large private companies realised the benefits offered by having direct labour: Cadbury's and ICI, for example, had direct labour workforces.

The method of obtaining construction work is the same today as it was when capitalism began. The industry is dominated by private contractors who tender for work in both the private and public sector. This is known as the "contracting system". You would think this was the only way that building work could be carried out, but the establishment of DLOs proved another way is possible. They showed the limitations of the private sector, which is not only unable to supply the homes we need, but lurches from one financial crisis to another.

Health and Safety report reveals contempt for building workers lives

What a travesty of justice and disregard for the lives of construction workers, when a Health and Safety Executive report revealed that in 1976 that in 1975 there were 181 fatal accidents in the private construction sector, and that this rate had hardly varied over the previous 30 years.

They said that "on present trends it is predicted that over the next 10 years 2,000 building workers will die in their workplace".

The report also said that "a 45-year-old building labourer could not expect to live long past retirement, while a 45-year-old building manager could expect to live until they are 75".

Above are Manchester DLO Workers who in 1977 were marching against the cuts in their DLO.

A PROGAMME FOR ACTION

These are the nine demands agreed by the DLO stewards at the meeting in Manchester in August 1977:

1. To fight to extend Direct Works Departments and support others in defence of public industries.

2. To fight for the early implementation of the 'Reg Freeson' Bill on Local Authorities.

3. To fight for the reversal of the cuts in the building industry and the restoration of the cuts in public spending for building. To call for an expansion of the building programme to build for people and not for private profit, and to fight the growing unemployment in the industry.

4. Conference fully supports the claim of the trade unions at present tabled with the local authorities and the demand for 'one rate' for schemes of incentive payments which hold production and earning down to 33 per cent and demand that these be replaced with union negotiated schemes.

5. To demand the rescinding by an act of parliament of the house of lord's decision that debars local authorities from the construction industry training board scheme of apprentice training.

6. To fight for the public ownership of the building industry and the building supply industry to end the price ringing and the monopoly price fixing of contract tenders.

7. To demand that all local authorities employ their own labour forced direct and end subcontracting of council building and maintenance contracts.

8. To demand that a national union membership agreement (UMA) apply within local authorities.

9. Conference calls for a national campaign involving full union agreed campaign procedures including local and national lobbies of council and parliament. The setting up of local action committees involving tenants, ratepayers, councillors and members of parliament, in addition to the trade union and labour movement. That a national committee of local authorities be organised with a view to a nationwide organisation to facilitate the implementation of the above aim.

In 1977, a conference was held in Manchester to fight to safeguard and extend DLOs that initiated a national campaign to expand direct works.

History of building Direct Labour Organisations

A nine-point programme was agreed on at the conference.

Below are some of the many examples of work that had been left unfinished by the contractors that had to be taken over and completed by DLOs in the 1970s. In many of the cases the standard of work left by the private builders had been so bad that work of the DLOs had to be started from scratch: (16)

Sandwell in 1977, Kelly homes went bankrupt, having finished only seven of the contracts of 80 houses at Union Street, Smethwick. When the DLO started work on completing the scheme, they found houses without foundations and drains, and sewers not properly connected.

Glasgow in 1975, the DLO took over a contract for a school and a housing estate of 199 houses.

Mansfield Liquidation of contractors meant the DLO has taken over two housing contracts which required a total of £47,000 in remedial work in 1979.

GLC The Grahame Park Estate in Hendon, taken over in 1974, is just one example of 15 contracts taken by the DLO with the spate of bankruptcies following the collapse of the property boom.

Manchester Livesey Street. A contract of 172 dwellings was left half-finished when the private builder went broke. The DLO completed the work within the contract period in 1978 at a saving of £15,818.

Sheffield Defects to five old people's homes taken over have meant that the completion of the building has taken as long as it would have done for the DLO to have started them from the beginning: the extra cost was estimated at £500,000.

Lambeth The DLO took over 50% of four contracts left unfinished because of bankruptcy, the contracts amounted to a total 690 new houses and 120 improvements.

Stoke-On-Trent Several contracts taken over, in addition to a £1m swimming pool in 1978.

Hammersmith in 1977, the DLO took over 12 contracts worth £100,000 from contractors who had gone bust.

Southwark

In 1978, contractors failed to complete 432 homes due to them going into liquidation. Contractor M.J. Shanley's liquidation cost the council then £240,000 in overspend. Much of the bankrupt contractor's work was completed by the councils own new build DLO "Southwark Construction."

History of building Direct Labour Organisations

Public-sector building DLOs have always been constrained (with some rare exceptions) by the lack of support from their Local Authority councillors and governments of the day. Private-sector building employers were always hostile towards local authority DLOs, because they feared having to compete against DLOs who were not based on their 'profit above all else' motive. They have a completely deregulated employment structure in the private sector of the construction industry, allowing them to act as they like. They succeeded in preventing the Labour Party from seriously considering the operation of a public national construction company by setting up the organisation named "Campaign against Building Industry Nationalisation" (CABIN) in the late 1970s. (32)

Above: can be seen a protest by GLC construction branch workers who were demonstrating against the cuts that led up to its closure in the late 1970s by Horace Cutler, leader of the then majority Tory GLC.

At the time the GLC employed over 1,000 directly employed workers and was one of the largest DLOs in the London area. Well-known leading construction trades unionist, fighter and friend "Tommy Finn" can be seen in the front, third from the right.

History of building Direct Labour Organisations

The overall number of building workers in DLOs was maintained in 1960s but in the 1970s, any expansion never came easy as many councils were reluctant to develop anything other than small emergency building works sections.

Even those councils that were more likely to set up large building DLOs had only done so because of much pressure from their tenants who were fed up with the shoddy work done by contractors.

Most senior managers of DLOs have been recruited from the private sector. Most of these managers have always been blinded with an obsession to get work done on time and at the cheapest cost possible with little consideration given to provide long-lasting quality work. They also brought with them the culture of exploitation and abuse of workers that existed in the private sector of the construction industry. With some rare exceptions, this meant these managers weren't capable of successfully promoting the full potential of the DLOs

The major gains made by DLO workers were achieved by having good working relations with tenants and councillors. That is when we succeeded in creating large numbers of direct labour jobs, got improvements to tenants' services, and good pay and working conditions for our members.

Yet, unlike building workers who had to fight to achieve better pay and conditions, management's pay and conditions were guaranteed as regular pay. It was only in the 1980s that most building workers and other manual workers were recognised as permanent employees of councils. But even so, we still have very low levels of basic pay. Before the mid-1980s were discriminated against by having to work a whole year before being allowed into the council's pension scheme.

Even now most DLO construction workers are still discriminated against when after many years of service, at the time of retirement, your pension would generally be smaller than officers, as a large part of the pension would depend on your productive pay that would be tied to the unpredictable levels of supply of work.

Also, most construction workers' productivity and consequently their productivity pay will be less on the last year before they retire. This then penalised these workers because of the effect of the many years of hard physical work they endure. Up until recently it was the last year's pay that was then used to calculate what will be a greatly reduced pension which they receive for the rest of their lives. (21)

History of building Direct Labour Organisations

Building workers employed in councils had pitiful low national basic pay rates, and still do. But pay increasingly begun to change when most councils began to introduce bonus schemes to drive up the productivity of their workers. This enabled DLO workers to earn more pay, but it also came at a price because it was a mechanism in which exploitation is increased by continually having to work harder and harder.

Management continually tried to replace bonus schemes with others that have far less generous bonus targets. They did this initially by setting up work-study or time and motion study departments, an idea brought from America, to increase productivity in Britain's factories. Councils wasted large amounts of taxpayer's' money in setting up and operating these work-study units. Lists of lower times for carrying out work would be produced on the false premise that this would increase productivity levels. Instead it produced the opposite, low levels of morale and even lower levels of productivity.

Then and today a far better incentive could be produced for DLO workers, ones that produce better quality work, rather than having productivity times which were impossible to achieve. Work levels could be maintained and increased if based on fair assessment of times required to do a job.

The discrimination against construction workers in DLOs by using these productivity schemes should come to an end and instead, they should be replaced by having all pay included into a salaried wage.

Some lower level managers could be more supportive of their workers' and trade union activity if they had previously come through the ranks and had been apprenticed to be trained as fully qualified tradespersons. These managers then have had the same experiences and so could appreciate the hard-working conditions in which building workers carried out their jobs.

Increasingly DLOs suffered from the introduction of vastly expensive private sector management consultants. These were brought in to give advice or even to run DLOs and these disastrous practices continue today.

Who needs contractors in social or private sector housing when DLOs can do much better?

Workers employed by contractors have no loyalty to them. Why should they, when they have no guarantees whatsoever on pay and conditions?

History of building Direct Labour Organisations

These workers are subject to all sorts of exploitation and insecurities, many without pension schemes, no sick or holiday pay, at the risk of being transferred at a moment's notice to other work, which can be a very long distance from their homes, work with little or no compliance with health and safety, and welfare standards. Many contractors at various times would hold back workers' pay and, in some cases, literally "do a runner" with their wages

In Southwark, and in most other councils, most workers employed by contractors would not live in the area where they worked, whereas most directly employed council workers did. This began to change in the 1990s when Southwark DLO senior managers and most councillors were too busy trying to run down the DLO to concern themselves with employing local council workers.

Those DLO workers employed locally prior to the 1970s would more likely put up with the low pay knowing they did not have to travel long distances to get to work. But this led to problems in getting building workers to apply for work in DLOs when more work became available from private contractors in the building boom years of the 1960-1970s.

This reluctance to work for DLOs was further compounded by the 1972 building workers' strike which pushed up private-sector workers' weekly wages by a minimum of £6, with many site workers being able to get further increases to their bonus and other rates of pay.

I can remember how difficult it was for Southwark Council to recruit skilled workers in 1975. When at our DLO head offices we regularly had 20 to 30 building workers taken on every Monday morning, but by the end of the week most of these workers had left.

Many that applied to work in the DLO were older construction workers who had worked hard all their lives and wanted to be able to slow down a bit in their later years, having gained a false impression from the media that council work was a cosy number, only to discover they had to work very hard for very little pay.

They would be frustrated by many things such as much travelling around the borough without always getting access to properties and having to placate tenants who wanted more work done than the council would allow. Added to this were the normal leavers, those from retirement age.

The cumulative effect was that the council had no net gain in its numbers. This slowly began to change as the benefits of having regular local employment, less travel, and council pension schemes becoming more available to the manual side began to attract a steady supply of skilled workers.

History of building Direct Labour Organisations

Also, the fight to better the pay and conditions of building DLO workers had increased when many trade union activists started to work in them. Many were forced to do so because they could not find work in the private sector. This wasn't because work levels had decreased, but because of the blacklisting activities of the employers that followed the 1972 building workers' strike and the Shrewsbury "conspiracy" trials.

The private sector does not invest in training of apprentices and if it does, it's training is of lower quality. Other than in the electrical and some other smaller trades that are subject to stricter safety standards the industry has become largely deregulated. An employer can go to a college and in effect buy the type of training they want. They now pass out an apprentice as qualified in a much shorter time than the days when an apprentice had three to four years' training. Apprentices are also being used as cheap labour. The current rate is £3.90 per hour (as of April 2019). This rate is for an apprentice in their first year of training regardless of age.

Today we see enormous sums being spent on either repairing bad quality work or having council housing demolished, for the sole purpose of making the property speculators and construction companies mega-rich.

Bovis Homes, one of the largest housebuilders in Britain announced in February 2017 they would pay £7m to repair poorly built new homes sold to customers, raising questions about the standards of new-build properties across the country and the regulation of the market. The news came amid growing complaints about the "National House Building Council" (NHBC) which provides a 10-year warranty for most new homes in Britain and sets the standards for new-build properties. (21)

Why can't we have Direct Labour Organisations set up in the private sector? The DLO system of work is a better way of organising to carry out the work for the homes we need. DLOs ensure better quality work that requires less subsequent repairs and maintenance. They are intended as a service; therefore, they are more sensitive to the disruption which building, and repair work can cause to tenants.

If they could be expanded into the private sector, the lower cost of their work can be used to lower the rents of tenants or costs to homeowners. For local authorities, this provides a cheaper and more efficient service, since they do not operate to make a profit and are accountable in terms of cost.

History of building Direct Labour Organisations

Why do we need to have this largely unregulated private building sector motivated only by the desire to make large profits for construction companies and which continually drives up the costs of housing?

It is construction workers who have the main responsibility for carrying out the fight for DLOs. These workers have the direct knowledge to educate and convince the communities that private contractors are no good for them, with their:

- price rigging and contract rigging
- their hostility towards trade unions and its blacklisting of union reps
- aversion towards employment of workers on decent terms and conditions
- greater costs
- less motivated workers
- work of poor-quality and design
- lack of local youth being trained through apprenticeships
- fewer skilled workers
- greater numbers of serious unsafe incidents, the exposure of workers and tenants to deadly dusts such as asbestos

With such arguments we can reverse the decline of DLOs that has taken place over the last 30-40 years. This can only be done with the recognition that our struggle is a political one.

Our struggle for building companies in the private sector to directly employ workers is of equal importance.

We should also not forget our demands for the establishment of a national public construction organisation so that we can act to end the monopoly control by the private sector of the building industry.

It is predicted that a crisis in supply of skilled construction workers in the UK is likely to get worse as we could lose 175,000 EU construction workers, or 8% of the sector's workforce, if the country does not retain access to the European single market after Brexit. (23)

We need to prepare now for an expansion of skilled workers so they can be employed in DLOs to meet the crisis of unavailable skilled labour.

Women in DLOs

Dr Christine Wall and Linda Clarke gave excellent contributions on "The history of DLOs & trades-women in DLOs" at the seminar I attended on 13th July 2017 entitled "DIRECT LABOUR PAST AND PRESENT". They said:

"Women have been a small part of the construction industry in relatively small numbers, except when they increased because of the lack of readily available skilled men during the 1st and 2nd world wars. Women had been employed in most construction trades with the largest numbers in painting and carpentry. It was only in 1941 that agreement was reached between employers and unions over how women would be paid. This was at basic rates of pay which were 20% less than the male rate of pay. By 1945 women employed in construction had risen to 24,200, 3.8%.

In the Second World War a conference was held by women working in the industry which demanded that they continue in their jobs in reconstruction and trade unions change their rules and practices to enable the employment of women trainees. However, despite a huge demand for reconstruction women were refused recruitment into the skilled trades, this despite the skills they had obtained during the war years. Yet again women were directed into what was considered as their traditional roles.

The construction craft unions restricted membership for those who had undertaken apprenticeships, this then acted to bar women from entry into work. At the time the electricians' trade union was more receptive to women workers.

Men could become antagonistic to women entering skilled jobs when women showed they were capable of doing what was men's traditional work during the two world wars.

Also, this was because women were being exploited as a source of cheap labour by employers. This was despite the TUC having supported equal pay for women since the 1890s.

The Training Opportunity Programme (TOPS) that provided six-month, intensive training courses in skill centres under industrial conditions was a boost to women obtaining construction skills as they were then classed as skilled workers.

In 1975, the Women and Manual Trades (WAMT) was set up. In 1982 the construction union UCATT set up a working party to monitor women in the industry and raised the issue of equal opportunities.

Women in DLOs

In the early 1980s Southwark and Lambeth set up Women's Training Workshops, with an introductory six-month course, financed with the help of the European Social Fund (ESF). Many women went on these adult training schemes. In 1989, 266 women were working in seven inner-London DLOs.

The 1985, Margaret Thatcher's government begun to reverse this progress when it scrapped the GLC and by the late 1980s reduced the powers of local authorities, including their ability to build new houses. The effect was to curb the activities of DLOs; as a result, many closed, and those which remained have been reduced to carrying out repair and maintenance operations; the adult trainee schemes collapsed. The operative workforce of DLOs was reduced from 238,000 in 1970 to 86,000 by 1995. The number of women employed in the seven DLOs was reduced from 266 in 1989, to only 64 by the early 1990s.

Nevertheless, the legacy of the systems set up in the 1980s survived, albeit in reduced form. Despite the attacks on their very existence, the local authority DLOs continued to train and maintain high quality training schemes". (24)

The Southwark Women's Workshop was established in the 1980s. The then Leader of the Council who was also a UCATT member was Ann Mathews; she was a major influence in getting this workshop opened. It offered six-month carpentry courses for women. It was officially opened by Tessa Sanderson the 1984-Olympics woman Javelin champion. I was involved in supporting the setting up of the workshop, and on some of the interview panels for the teaching instructors and involved in induction training.

Many women went from the workshop to become adult carpenter apprentices in Southwark and other DLOs in London. At its height, Southwark DLO had over twenty adult women tradesperson's all members of trades unions, with their own shop steward.

Southwark Council Direct Labour Organisation

Historical Timeline to Southwark DLO History

1900s. Southwark became one of the earliest public-sector housing authorities in the London area to set up its own new build DLO - after the London County Council (LCC). The Spa Road estate was one of the earliest new builds carried out by Bermondsey council which directly employed workers.

1900-1940s. The four boroughs that now comprise Southwark: Bermondsey, Walworth, Camberwell and Peckham had always carried out day-to-day housing repairs by DLOs to some degree and in one form or another.

1950-1970. Various new-build operations by its DLO included East Dulwich Road, Cheltenham Road and the largest, the North Peckham estate.

1965. Southwark Construction was the new build division that emerged from the council's own previous new build department. The difference was this DLO was run by a small team of managers from Bovis. Southwark Construction closed in 1980 with many of its workers transferred to the council's other building DLO, the Housing Works Division. (30)

1980s. The closure of Inner London Education Authority (ILEA) and the Greater London Council (GLC) led to the transfer of over 170 building workers that increased Southwark's Housing by a third; Southwark also took over the ILEA schools in the borough, all of which had to be maintained. (27)

2019. There are plans to merge what's left of Housing works, Highways, and Environmental Services Maintenance into one DLO together with a purpose-built depot. By 2019 the council had taken back all its repairs and maintenance work to its in house DLO.

My own history with Southwark Building DLO

From construction, private sector to working for Southwark DLO

I suffered from being blacklisted prior to starting work with Southwark Council. This was confirmed in 2009 when the Government's data protection organisation the "Information Commissioner's Office" raided the organisation named as "The Consultancy Association". It was then that we found most of the evidence about over 3,200 building workers who had been blacklisted. It was no wonder that trades unions have always found it so difficult to achieve good union-organised sites in the private sector when so many trade union activists were denied employment because of blacklisting. (25)

My own history with Southwark Building DLO

When I left the contractor John Laing's in 1975, I was surprised to get an immediate start with Southwark council's Housing Works Division DLO. I started work with Southwark on its Tyre's Estate site in July 1975. It was then that the council had launched a huge modernisation programme for its inter-war estate properties. My aim in working for Southwark was the same as being employed anywhere else, which was to achieve better standards of pay, safety and other improvements in working conditions.

But none of this come comes out of thin air, it comes with struggle. This can be summed up by a great slogan from the early days of the trade union movement which is: "Agitate, Organise and Educate". The tried and tested instinct for me and many trade union activists which I learned from working with over 20 contractors in the private sector was first to keep your head down, work hard, making sure your work was of the best quality and to try and be at work on time. You had to earn the respect of the workers on the job, but just as important you must try not to give management any excuse to sack you. I would also have to try and suss out who amongst my fellow workers were friendly towards our trade unions. This was so I could rely on them in defeating any sort of backlash from management while I was making progress in forming solid trade union organisation on the job. It was no easy task when you always had someone amongst you who would act as a "grass" and report back union activity to management.

What was common in those days in DLOs was to take on workers directly on site. This involved a brief interview with some trades, and questions being asked. If successful, you would be taken on the following day and then given work that tested your ability to do the job. In my case I was asked to make a "saw-horse." This was a narrow but strong and well-balanced work platform used by carpenters to carry out their work on site. Making a saw-horse tested a person's ability to construct a well-designed structure and make use of their skills by having the correct angle joints required. I passed the test.

Work on Tyres Estate involved the complete overhaul of these properties as did the large programme of work on all the Bermondsey and Rotherhithe inter-war estates. I was about to pack in the job after being employed for only two days when I found out how low the productivity pay targets were for me to earn any money. You relied on making a bonus to earn a reasonable wage because of a very low basic rate of pay. The council had imposed impossible bonus targets which were based on a so-called work study evaluation. These involved a person standing over you with a specially designed stopwatch, a writing pad and a tape recorder.

My own history with Southwark Building DLO

The work carried out by a work study officer was to record every aspect of how you did the job, and then come up with the productivity time allowed to do that work.

Luckily for me I was convinced by another carpenter who was named Ron Herbert, to stay. Ron said to me he would help me get this rectified by persuading the workers on this site to put pressure on management to get the bonus rates changed. It was no surprise that management's response to our complaints was to offer work-study exercises. Because of the growing opposition to these unfair bonus rates I decided to volunteer to be work-studied. I relished the thought of trying to beat them at their own game.

I was successful at being work-studied, was soon elected the carpenters' shop steward and quickly earned a reputation for achieving better bonus targets. The trick was to know your subject far better than the person who was carrying out the work study exercise, ensure every aspect of the job is fully timed, insist that sufficient time allowances are made for things such as rest periods, interruptions from others, that a good quality product is produced, full safe working practices are carried out and any unforeseen circumstances are allowed for.

I also gained support after attracting some publicity when I refused to hang a window that involved me having to lean towards the outside of a second floor flat without first having the protection of a scaffold. There were some things I could not fix, when one day management complained that they would have to dismiss a painter apprentice for continuously being late and absent from work.

It was what happened the following day which was the last straw for management. I went to do work on what was supposed to be an empty flat, but found it locked from the inside, and because time was getting on, I had to report this to the site charge hand, who then carried out a forced entry to the door. To our complete surprise, when we got inside, we discovered the apprentice together with what appeared to be his girlfriend on the floor rolled up into the painter's dustsheets. It was obvious from the look on their faces they had had a few drinks the night before and had very much enjoyed their own company.

A year later, this story was met with some amusement from my fellow workers when they learned that after leaving Southwark this same apprentice had completed his apprenticeship with a private company, and then got employed back again on Southwark Building DLO as a fully time-served tradesperson.

My own history with Southwark Building DLO

After being with Southwark for nine months a meeting was scheduled to be held of all Southwark building trades stewards so that they could elect a new convenor. This was to replace the then convenor, Fred Stansbury who was due to retire as he was over 65. A fellow carpenter steward from an inter-war estate site in downtown Rotherhithe, a great man named Denis Everett, spoke to me before the meeting and asked if he could nominate me for the position. Denis originally came from Barbados and had previously experienced trade union struggles in that country.

The meeting was held at the old Walworth Road Town Hall. The UCATT regional organiser Jack Kennedy was present as were 25 shop stewards from different construction trades unions. These shop stewards represented all the various sites and maintenance depots of the council. I was nominated by a bricklayer steward from a major conversion site at Grosvenor Terrace whose name was Les Wilkes. Another two people, Denis Shanahan, a carpenter steward on the Marcia Road conversion site and Allen Coe, a plumber from day to day maintenance at Spa Road depot, were also nominated. Allen declined nomination and I was then elected with a two-thirds majority over Denis Shanahan.

I was surprised, but very excited at being elected after only being on the council for nine months, with hardly any experience about the day-to-day maintenance operations of the council. I was born and brought up in Southwark from a trade union-minded family of mainly building trade workers. So, I was proud to be the leader who would be representing the council's building trade unions. I knew I had a big responsibility to fight to maintain and advance the livelihoods of over 700 workers and I was then was just 27 years of age. I could never have imagined then that I would serve in this position for the next 37 years until I retired.

Fred Stansbury, the convenor I took over from was an old-style Labour Party supporter who had been a staunch trade unionist all his life. But Fred was not in the best of health, having very bad knees meant he could not get around to visit workers as much as he would have liked.

Visiting workers was an essential part of trying to establish a thriving trade union organisation. Being able to do so was not easy when there were at any one time up to 30 building sites, many depots and other locations. We also had 150 painters who hardly needed to go to depots as they were visited daily by 15 painter chargehands at council flats or houses and at external painting sites.

Added to this, many workers who were new employees had to be seen due to the large turnover of DLO employees.

My own history with Southwark Building DLO

Fred should have seen these workers on their first day at work to ensure they were in a union, but because of his bad health this did not always happen. This meant the recruitment of workers into the trade union suffered. It was true to say that at the time about 30%, or 210 of the 700 DLO workers were not in a trade union. This wasn't because they didn't want to join, but simply because they had not been asked.

To rectify this, my priorities then were to:

1. Be at the main building DLO office early in the morning on the first day so the new starters that were being taken on could be immediately signed up to the union.

2. Visit all the painters to inform them of our trade union activities.

3. Visit sites and depots, holding meetings with gangs, and have individual meetings for those not in the union. At that time, all new members had to pay a membership fee to join. This meant that on some occasions I had to make another visit to collect this fee. All in all, the drive to achieve 100% trade union membership took up a large part of my time over the next three years.

I never had any problems with workers not wanting to join the union other than three individuals. One said it was against his religious beliefs because he was a Jehovah's Witness. The second said that he did not want to join because he had been let down previously by the unions. The third refused to join because he supported the ideas of the National Front. The first worker eventually joined after he found that other workers of the same religious views were already union members. The second worker was persuaded that unions don't aim to let down their members but sometimes we don't always win. The third worker was forced to leave because the plumbers in our DLO refused to work with him.

Some of the attacks I faced in my 37 years with Southwark

I thought it important to have a section in this book with a brief description of some of the attacks I faced in the 37 years I had worked for Southwark Council as its building trades unions Convenor. I have done so because I know that every other dedicated union activist will have faced the same type of harassment and discrimination I had while working for a local authority DLO. We should not have to put up with this, and it's about time we acted to get guarantees that this won't happen in the future.

My own history with Southwark Building DLO

In 1975, As soon as I was elected as the union convenor, I was singled out for pay reductions. Although it was common practice to work on a Saturday morning, I was barred from doing so, and consequently lost 16% of my pay packet. It was only in 1984 when the political makeup of the council changed that I got this overturned.

Despite being elected in 1975, it was only in 1982 that the council agreed to recognise me as the full-time elected convenor. The building trade unions were the first to get this recognition from the council.

In 1977, I attended a site meeting of plumbers. There I discovered a member of the "National Front" who was not in our union. He was spouting all sorts of racist views. I ordered him to leave the meeting. He refused and decided to throw a punch at me. All the plumbers then refused to work with him, and he was forced to leave Southwark's employment.

In 1978, I was visited by roofing contractors at my office in Spa Road Depot. These contractors threatened me with violence because I had put pressure on management to remove contractors and replace them with directly employed council workers. Fortunate for me they backed down when I was able to convince some of them that the union's aim in getting workers directly employed would help to improve the conditions of all construction workers, whether they were employed with the council or with private sector contractors.

In May 1979, myself and the UCATT regional organiser Jack Kennedy and I were faced with violence when we did an inspection of the DLO conversion site in Braganza Street, Kennington. We later found out that this man was the director of a small roofing subcontractor named (would you believe) GBH. This contractor was left in no doubt about how trade unions respond to attacks on their representatives when the following day he was forced off the job by our own direct labour workers who descended in large numbers to put picket lines on this site. (26)

Between 1981-2005, as well as the discrimination I had already suffered over my wages, management refused to update my pay in line with other workers'. I was denied any increase in my pay when all other DLO building workers had the one-third maximum productivity pay limit Increased to two-thirds of the basic rate of pay and by 1985 the cap was removed completely. It was only in 2006 that I could get this rectified.

In 1990, management arbitrarily decided to remove my car allowance payments which I had received since its introduction in 1985.

My own history with Southwark Building DLO

For the second time, in September 1994, I took this matter to an industrial tribunal. To my joy, I won the case. However, management won their appeal because the mileage allowance was not (they said) wages, but expenses. The judge however, said that: "He agreed with me that the decision to stop this payment in his view constituted discrimination against me as I was solely picked out from hundreds of other workers for this deduction".

In July 1995. I was told I was to be transferred over to a contractor, under the Transfer of Undertakings (Protection of Employment) Regulations, 1981 (TUPE), and at the same time my release for carrying out trade union duties would be withdrawn. I made a formal complaint of discrimination and harassment. It was only after UCATT issued a letter from their solicitors threatening an injunction that management backed down, but only to give me a notice of redundancy. I applied to the industrial tribunal for interim relief, while UCATT held a ballot for industrial action. Again, management backed down.

In May 2004, I wrote to Southwark management to tell them that my doctor had informed me that x-rays showed I had an asbestos-related medical condition called "pleural plaques". I provided a statement showing that Southwark had polluted me with asbestos dust and followed this up by taking out a successful claim with the UCATT solicitor for compensation.

In June 2010, I received a letter stating I would no longer be allowed full-time release to carry out my duties as the convenor. I responded by writing to the council's senior human resources officer, stating the historic facts relating to my employment with Southwark. Then In July 2010 I met with the senior human resources officer together with Chris Tiff, the UCATT regional organiser, and with some determination by us we got management to back down from their position.

The make-up of Southwark DLO's workforce

Like many DLOs throughout the UK, Southwark in the 1970s had a huge new-build housing programme. Some of its work was carried out by its own direct labour workforce with most carried out by some of the largest construction companies in the country. It also had a large conversion and rehabilitation programme for existing council properties.

It had two separate building works divisions: one was "Southwark Construction" (SC) which carried out new building works and the other was the "Housing Works Division" (HWD) The HWD did large council housing conversions, improvement, rehabilitation, planned day-to-day repairs, emergency works and maintenance programs.

The make-up of Southwark DLO's workforce

Southwark also had another Direct Labour Organisation that mainly carried out minor and major renewals and maintenance of its roads, pavements, street lighting and parks.

The HWD had approximately 175 workers engaged on its day-to-day and emergency works which operated out of two large depots: one at Copeland Road in Peckham and the other in Spa Road, Bermondsey. There were also several much smaller depots. Our 150 painters were based in the Spa Road depot, but in the main started work each day from homes of tenants, unoccupied properties and external painting programmes. These painters were mostly engaged in the summer in huge programmes to paint external wooden doors and windows and communal areas. The replacement of wooden doors and windows with more weather-proof UPVC-coated aluminium brought about a rapid decline in the numbers of painters employed in Southwark DLO and others throughout the country.

Above is a picture of part of Southwark DLOs largest depot at Copeland Road in 1982.

The make-up of Southwark DLO's workforce

Southwark conversion and improvement sites were scattered all around the borough. Between 1970-1980 the largest sites were the numerous inter-war estate improvement sites in Rotherhithe and Bermondsey, and the conversion sites at Grosvenor Terrace, Marcia Road and Devon Mansions. These sites had combined numbers of up to 400 directly employed council building workers.

SC DLO new-build sites division had up to 450 directly employed council workers at any one time and was managed by a team from the contractor Bovis Ltd. The Council originally brought them in as management consultants in 1968 following a scandal being discovered involving the projects manager on the North Peckham project, who was dismissed. The North Peckham Estate was a huge development which started in the 1960s and continued into the 1970s. Only carpenters, bricklayers and labourers were engaged as Southwark Council directly employed workers, all other trades work was subcontracted. (30)

This contrasted with the Council's "Housing Works Division" which had some of its work subcontracted, but nevertheless did most of its work using its own directly employed workers. The DLO employed workers who were highly qualified, being able to carry out all necessary trades work that was required towards the council's properties.

The Housing Works DLO had at various times, many workshops, which built its own building products. Our largest workshops were based in Spa Road, Copeland Road and Frensham Street depots. The activities carried out from these workshops included: wood-mill machinery activities, production of various joinery items, painting, glazing, metal fitting welding and prefabrications, scaffolding storage and maintenance, vehicle maintenance and repair.

After the GLC transfers we had many other smaller depots transferred to us. Work from these depots allowed our apprentices to gain much needed skills and experience which would not otherwise have been available.

The make-up of Southwark DLO's workforce

Above is our wood-mill and painting workshop at Copeland Road in 1982.

The make-up of Southwark DLO's workforce

The council closed Southwark Construction in November 1980 and about 20 of their direct labour workforce agreed to transfer to the Housing Works Division. In 1986, the Tory government abolished the Greater London Council (GLC), which meant that over 150 building workers were transferred to us. This was followed with the abolition of the Inner London Education Authority (ILEA) in 1990 which transferred a further 20 workers to our DLO. The transfers enabled us to negotiate the best aspects of either Southwark's or the GLC and ILEA productivity bonus schemes. Southwark Construction bonus scheme was not used as new-build work was not comparable to the type of work we carried out. Some parts of the ex-GLC and ILEA workers' contracts that weren't compatible with Southwark's operations were bought out. The combined workforce that came over enabled us to strengthen our trade union organisation and our stewards' committee numbers increased from 30 to over 50. (27)

The DLO took on thousands of young apprentices between 1975 and 1990-at any one time over 100 apprentices were employed. They were encouraged to extend themselves and obtain high levels of skill and qualifications, some would win national and regional competitions as the best apprentices. Most apprentices after serving their time would continue to work in the DLO. Many became DLO supervisors, managers and housing officer managers.

In addition to the trades workers there were large numbers of officer and management workers within DLOs. These numbers varied but could add up to a quarter towards the overall numbers who worked for DLOs. While Southwark Construction closed in 1980, Southwark Housing Works Division DLO continued to operate, and still does, albeit with hugely reduced numbers since then, as well as undergoing several changes of name. The highest point was in 1983 when it had over 1,300 building trades workers. Its numbers had been reduced to 882 by 1990 when it had 38 shop stewards of whom 25 were safety reps. Our unions then were UCATT, EEPTU, TGWU, GMB, and MSF. By January 2011 only 140 building workers were still working. In 2017 its numbers fluctuated at around 100. In July 2019, because all repairs are done by the DLO, its numbers have increased to 142.

The Highways DLO has been reduced from employing up to 200 workers in 1978 to 20 trades and associated skilled workers in 2019.

The decline of numbers employed in our DLOs over the last 30 to 40 years was the same throughout the country, and in some cases, it was even worse, with many DLOs being completely closed and their work being taken over by private contractors.

The make-up of Southwark DLO's workforce

The Transfer of Undertakings (Protection of Employment) Regulations (TUPE) regulations were introduced by the EEU in 1981.

They were first used in Southwark in 1993 after several attempts made by the government to oppose them in other workplaces. These TUPE regulations allowed approximately 50 workers in our DLO to be transferred to contractors between 1993-1999.

In 2011, management was successful in reducing our DLO workers by enticing them to accept voluntary redundancies. We had prevented even further job losses after being successful in persuading Jerry Scott, then Director of Housing, to look at the possibility of starting up our own teams to take some of the subcontractors' work back to our DLO. We took part in joint reviews to ascertain whether we could carry out works involving major drain clearance, asbestos removal, scaffolding, an extended joinery workshop, and damp specialist treatment. This enabled us to obtain damp elimination and drain clearance work and maintaining a limited joinery and woodcutting facility.

Our Links with others

We have been involved in many direct actions to oppose the employers' and the government's attacks such as those on the miners, health workers, print workers, dockers, seafarers and others as we were also linked to the wider community and its campaigning activities over the struggles concerned with social justice issues.

Some of those we were closely involved with included:

- UCATT Joint Stewards' Branch Officers' Organisation for South East London.
- London Building Convenors' Committee for Local Authority DLOs.
- London Bridge organisation.
- Anti-rate capping organisation the- "Crisis in London Campaign".
- Local and national "Defend Council Housing" organisations.'
- Construction Safety Campaign.
- UCATT Broad Left.
- Justice for Shrewsbury Pickets campaign.
- Southwark against the Poll Tax campaign.
- Southwark Group of tenants' organisations.

Our Links with others

- Southwark Trades Council.

- SERTUC Public Services Committee.

- Blacklist Support Group.

- London Hazards Centre.

- Southwark Pensioners Action Group.

We were in the leadership of the "London DLO convenors' committee" and the "London Bridge" public sector stewards' organisation which had quite an impact in the 1980s as it led many combined actions including strike action over the closures of ILEA and the GLC. The London DLO Convenors' Committee facilitated negotiations between the different councils' DLO shop steward committees and had a strong united position when faced with negotiation with management over the transfers. We were at the time able to obtain funding from Ken Livingstone, then mayor of the GLC, so that we could finance our own regular publication that was entitled 'Local Authority News'.

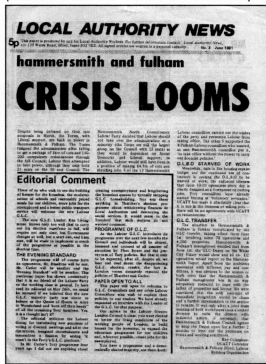

See above the front page of the June 1998 Local Authority News.

Our Links with others

The 1985 Housing Act allowed tenants to vote and set up 'Housing Action Trusts.' This had wide implications for tenants, housing workers and DLOs and was the first major privatisation initiative of Southwark Councils Housing.

Our shop stewards' committee vigorously opposed the setting up of a Trust on the North Peckham and Gloucester Grove estates in Central Peckham. At the time, we produced several thousand cards which spelt out the reasons why tenants should oppose the move to privatise their estates and distributed these to every home on these estates.

A H.A.T. OR A HOME?

Government has decided to set up a Housing Action Trust (H.A.T.) in Southwark, to take over Council estates and prepare them for ownership by private landlords for profit. H.A.T.s will only exist for a short period — until the properties have been sold off.

H.A.T.s will initially be funded by grants from the Government to do repairs and improvements (money that the Government has cut from the Council's budget to stop it from carrying out the repairs and maintenance it wants to).

Under the new Housing Bill the Government states that it is giving the right to private landlords to take over your estates.

HAS ANYONE GIVEN YOU A CHOICE?

IF A H.A.T. TAKES OVER YOUR ESTATE HOW WILL YOU BE AFFECTED?

■ Rent increases.
■ Lack of housing for people on low incomes.
■ No say in who your estate is sold to.
■ No say in how your estate is run.
■ Loss of local jobs.
■ Possible eviction to make a profit.
■ No guarantee of repairs being done.
■ No option to return to the Council.
■ If you die or move your children could not take over the tenancy as they can with the Council.
■ Increased homelessness.

PROTECT YOURSELF AND YOUR HOME, SAVE YOUR ESTATE, SAY NO TO H.A.T.S.

Published by LBS Building Workers Shop Stewards Committee

See the leaflets we distributed above:

Tenants had raised several concerns with Harriet Harman, the MP for Camberwell and Peckham. The outcome of this resistance from tenants' organisations was that most councils including Southwark, were unable to establish Housing Action Trusts. (28)

Between 1991- 1993, we supported the "Crisis in London Campaign." This campaign aimed to unite all those involved in struggles over the poll tax, deaths at work, the unemployed, pensioners and many other issues.

Our Links with others

SOME 60 members from a wide range of organisations attended the Crisis in London Campaign's annual general meeting at the Conway Hall, Holborn, last Saturday.

Transport workers, engineers, building workers, local government workers, teachers, workers in the health service, and civil servants were among those at the conference who decided on a programme of action for the campaign, and elected its officers for the coming year.

A wide-ranging discussion about the problems hitting millions of Londoners, in the midst of the deepening economic and social crisis, had contributions from members of the National Union of Journalists, the Equity actors' union, a delegate from Hither Green Labour Party, pensioners' organisations, the Unemployed Workers' Charter, Kurdish refugees, those involved in the fight against the poll tax, and Haringey, Lambeth, Tower Hamlets, Bexley and Camden trades councils, and Labour MP Jeremy Corbyn.

Above is a picture and an account of a meeting of this campaign held in February 1992. Jeremy Corbyn MP, now leader of the Labour Party, was for many years a supporter of the campaigns we were involved with. Jeremy was a speaker at this meeting. In the picture can be seen from left to right Liz Leicester, Ed Hall and Tony O'Brien. Also shown are the organisations represented at this event.

Pay and conditions agreements of Southwark DLO

While local authority building DLOs have never been as bad as the private sector, none the less, it has always been a major struggle to achieve proper pay and conditions of employment. Bonus schemes have been the main mechanism used by management to prevent unity among DLO workers.

We always argued that bonus schemes should be replaced by a guaranteed decent wage, and we don't mean by this that it should be based on our union's very low national basic pay agreements. When I joined Southwark in July 1975, until 1979, there was a huge turnover of building workers who started work for Southwark and then left within just a few weeks. Southwark and many other local authority DLOs could not compete with the pay from the private sector of the construction industry. Some councils in London, such as Lewisham, did not even pay what was an even lower building worker London weighting allowance. Most, council's holiday leave entitlements were less, and in most cases holiday pay did not include the pay for all hours worked. You had to wait for a year before you could join the council's pension scheme.

We were not happy to rely on what were very precarious bonus schemes to try and boost our pay. These schemes' payments were capped. At the time, we continually raised the question of these inequalities. Finally, we began to make some progress when we reached agreement with the Labour councillors to establish a list of the issues, we felt discriminated against our members.

While throughout the country pay and conditions would vary from one DLO to another. All DLO workers were able to achieve major gains not possible in the private sector of construction. This was possible because we were able to reach out to obtain support from the tenants' movement and others over pay-inequality issues. This allowed us to achieve some of what other council officer workers already had: such as pensions, sick pay, holidays with pay, trade union recognition and better health and safety standards. Those DLOs who had better trade union organisation achieved even better pay and conditions that had been provided by our union's national negotiated agreements.

Over the many years I worked in Southwark we had numerous changes made to our members' pay and conditions of work. The following is a brief outline:

- 1979, we achieved a new council-wide standby allowance that would be paid equally for officers, building workers and manual workers.

Pay and conditions agreements of Southwark DLO

- A profit-sharing agreement was introduced into the housing conversions contracts side of our building DLO, with payments first made in 1980. In 1983, this was extended for all building workers within the DLO.

- In March 1985 we established the London Weighting parity agreement with officer workers. In later years, we got this London Weighting payment consolidated into our guaranteed minimum rate of pay.

- In 1985, the council set up a sub-contractor working party and invited us to take part. This gave us the opportunity to have many sub-contractors replaced by our own direct labour employed workers. The chair of this committee was the late councillor Danny McCarthy. Danny was a senior Labour councillor; who had previously been an electrician trade union activist in the private sector of the construction industry. Other councillors on this committee were also trade union activists and known for their principled stand over workers' rights. Namely, John Bryan Brian Kelly and Sandy McPherson

- In May 1985, we reached agreement on "service Increments equalisation". This allowed building workers to increase these payments in line with officer employees of the council and later they would be consolidated into our guaranteed minimum rates of pay.

- In July 1988, we reached agreement for the harmonisation and consolidation of annual holiday leave and the council's concessionary day's leave with the officer and manual workers of the council. This Increased building workers' holiday leave from a minimum of 26 days a year to a maximum of 29 days when long service leave was added.

- In 1989, we bought our first computer. We became one of the first workplace trade union organisations to use computer technology to advance our organisation's capabilities. With up to 50 shop stewards, the task of doing mail-outs, including the printing of address labels, became much easier and we had better quality leaflets produced for our members.

- On 5 July 1989 we got a major increase in pay when the plumbers' national basic rate of pay was agreed to be paid as the calculator for all the different trades' rates of pay.

- In 1990, we got back the out-of-normal working hours emergency call-out work previously given out to contractors.

Pay and conditions agreements of Southwark DLO

- In January 1994, we got the DLO's basic hourly week reduced from 39 to 37 hours, this was despite many on-going attacks that was taking place at this time to many of our other terms and conditions.

- In April 1997, we reached agreement on a revised scheme for emergency work being carried out outside normal working hours. This scheme enabled more DLO workers to be engaged in this type of work and was strengthened by the inclusion of the EU directives on working hours.

- In 1998, we had a new council-wide "Time off for Trade Union Duties" agreement.

- In 1998, we negotiated an agreement over the use of council vans for travel from work to home and from home to work.

- In June 2001, we reached agreement with highways' management that apprentices would be paid productivity payments from out of the tradesmen tender-led credits.

- In January 2002, we reached agreement on management's proposal for a new pay scheme based on moving away from pay centred solely on productivity to one that combined productivity with quality targets.

- In 2004, we reached agreement on the payment of a £10 per day contingency allowance for those who were involved in lower earnings levels of work.

- Between March and January 2004, Highways Management issued a notice of termination on our metal fitters' tender-led productivity pay. We got this turned around and secured an agreement that mirrored the guarantees already contained in the building DLO pay agreements

  We also obtained a reduction in basic hours from 37 to 36 hours.

- On April 2004, we agreed minimum job prices per trade with Chris Culleton the then Interim Building Manager for our Building DLO.

- In August 2004. we reached agreement on how apprentices who were in their last year could be involved in the productivity scheme if they had obtained at least a level two NVQ and had been assessed as reaching a high level of achievement.

- In March 2005, the metal fitters were transferred from the highways' DLO back to the building DLO. We successfully concluded an agreement on all the issues concerned with this transfer.

- In 2008, our guaranteed minimum rate of pay for a building tradesperson increased to £428.25p per week and a profit share payment of £236.00p was paid.

- In 2009, our guaranteed minimum rate of pay increased to £432.53p per week.

- For many years we got large discounts when our members bought tools through the DLO's stores very welcome when our members' tools were lost or stolen. In addition, our members could use the council's recreation centres' facilities at discounted prices

Disproportionate levels of management to DLO workers

Until 1991, the first line of direct management for our DLO workers was charge-hands. Work was carried out by individual gangs directly controlled by these building trade chargehands. All chargehands had worked their way up from being tradespersons, many were ex-shop stewards with organising abilities and the understanding of what a tradesperson's work problems were. Chargehands were paid a plus rate on top of their trade basic rate of pay. They got productivity pay based on their gang's average productivity output. So, they had an incentive to ensure that the tradespersons in their gang were efficiently managed and given immediate support when problems occurred. This was not the position with line managers who were salary-paid officers.

This method of directly managing building workers wasn't always the best, especially if the ratios between chargehands and tradespersons weren't correct. It was, however, much more of a hands-on approach to managing workers than having line managers.

For many years chargehands suffered from not having their contracts of employment revised to record that they were the immediate line managers of workers. This meant they did not have permanent positions and could easily be threatened with being put back on the tools. Most of these chargehands had been doing these jobs for many years. Being put back on the tools could be a serious risk to their health as well as involving a drop in their pay and a cut to their pension.

We eventually resolved this major dispute after the chargehands threatened industrial action.

The use of charge-hands ended in 1991 with a huge reduction of the DLO workforce. They were then given an offer of accepting voluntary redundancy or being given a new contract of employment as a first line manager.

Disproportionate levels of management to DLO workers

The number of these line managers was subsequently reduced over subsequent years, especially because of the introduction of mobile phones and their add-on technologies.

The work carried out by construction workers in DLOs suffered from large and disproportionate managerial on-costs. These costs were levied against operational costs and became part of the DLO trading accounts. If they were too high the viability of the DLO was under threat. These costs included: work-study officers, bonus department officers, contract surveyor officers, contract evaluating and monitoring officers and human resources officers. Some of the work carried out by these officers could be duplicated by officers in the Housing Department which was not part of the DLO. This meant that this work was done less efficiently. The overall effect was that less money was available for repair work, yet some of these officers were required. And while over the years some processes have become more efficient, a lot more could have been done, and done much sooner.

It's my experience that the reason for the disproportion of officers to building workers can largely be put down to a culture generated over many years by higher management that says: "Large numbers of managers are needed so as to have sufficient control over workers, who cannot be trusted". They felt that what management did was more important. This attitude of having too many chiefs and not enough Indians is wrong. It's wrong because it is the work done of hanging doors, putting in windows, the lighting, plumbing and all the other work of tradespersons that counts the most.

Over many years in Southwark when I came across managers who had this attitude of superiority and went out of the way to abuse their positions of authority, I had to remind them that the DLO could live without them, but the DLO would not exist without its tradespersons as it was they who carried out its main functions.

Our unions over many years were constantly involved in arguing for management to reduce their own on-costs instead of attacking our jobs and our terms and conditions of employment.

Later, our main problem was the council's use of private contract managers and consultants in our DLO.

The attacks on Southwark's Direct Labour Organisation and our response

Our DLO workers acted straight away after a decision was made in 1976 by delegates at UCATT's national conference to ban all asbestos products. UCATT followed this up by issuing a letter to all its shop stewards and safety reps saying: *"UCATT'S policy is, therefore, a total ban on the use of asbestos in all its forms."* Immediately after this, most of the DLO trade unions in London including Southwark, Hackney, Camden, and Islington put this ban into practice. In Southwark, we instructed our storemen to lock up what was then called "Asbestolux". This was an insulation board that management and the council's safety department had insisted had no asbestos properties in it. We did not believe them, so we refused management's instructions. (36)

In 1976 we held several days of solidarity action by not crossing picket lines put up by the dustmen at our Spa Road depot's building DLO entrance, when they were on strike over pay. We later found out that as part of the agreement to settle the industrial action, the dustmen would be paid the equivalent to what they had lost in strike days while working to remove the large backlogs of rubbish that had piled up. This resulted in many angry building DLO workers visiting my office to demand something be done, as while they lost pay for refusing to cross the picket lines the dustmen were boasting to them that they didn't lose anything.

I told these workers that I agreed with them and would resolve the issue. I then went to speak to the dustmen's stewards at the depot to explain our concerns. I said that we had no problem in not crossing the picket lines on our part of this depot, however, if they wanted us to continue to be part of their dispute we must be treated equally. That meant they had to be prepared to share with us any monies they got from their dispute to compensate us for any pay we lost in supporting them. If not, when we put up picket lines over our own disputes, we would also put them up on the Spa Road entrances that were used by their own dustcart vehicles.

The dustmen stewards understood the position and readily agreed that in the future, before they put up picket lines on any of the gates at the Spa Road depot, they would meet with us so that we could reach a joint agreement.

In 1977, a work-to-rule by plumbers was taking place in our Spa road and Copeland Road depots, as well as all our improvement sites.

The attacks on Southwark's Direct Labour Organisation and our response

This came about after provocative actions, and a violent attack was made on me by a non-union plumber.

Also, in 1977, large cutbacks and closures were beginning to take place in many other DLOs throughout the country. While this did not at that time affect us, our joint steward's committee met and decided to recommend support for a day of action called by the national building trade unions. We held a mass meeting on 18 July at the Spa Road depot library hall and voted to stop work the following day.

Below can be seen is our leaflet for this meeting:

What preceded these attacks was the national building employers increasingly moving away from direct employment and encouraging the use of lump labour by subcontractors.

The attacks on Southwark's Direct Labour Organisation and our response

They were fearful of the calls made by many trades union activists that the Labour Party should commit to setting up of a public-sector based "National Construction Company" especially when a campaign to nationalise the building construction Industry was raised as an issue at the 1977 Labour Party conference by the late Labour MP Eric Heffer.

The employers decided to counter-attack by setting up an organisation named "Campaign against Building Industry Nationalisation" (CABIN), to frighten and discredit any moves by Labour to set up a publicly controlled national building organisation. They added to the clamour from the Tories and those right wing, Liberals and Labour politicians who were hostile to DLOs.

Federation of Master Builders Campaign Against Direct Labour and Nationalisation

A Meeting will be held on Monday, the 17th April, 1978, at the Waldorf Hotel, Aldwych, W.C.2, commencing at 7 p.m.

Speaker: Michael Heseltine M.P., Shadow Secretary of the Environment
SUPPORTED BY CAMDEN COUNCILLORS

Camden Council places contracts with its Direct Labour Building Department to keep its staff employed. Its record speaks for itself.
Mansfield Road New Housing now in its fourth year and the completion nowhere in sight.

WHY SHOULD THE RATEPAYER CONTINUE TO SUBSIDISE DIRECT LABOUR ?
WHY PAY MORE FOR LESS? — WHY ACCEPT INEFFICIENCY ?

The Government's own figures indicate that private builders are 100 per cent more efficient than Direct Labour Building Departments.

Is there a successful Direct Labour Building Department in the U.K? Getting rid of Camden Direct Labour Building Department would, we believe, save the ratepayers up to 3p in the £.

Our comment to Camden Council: — YOU'VE TRIED. — YOU'VE FAILED. — NOW DISBAND IT
You cannot continue to paper over the cracks.

SUPPORT OUR FIGHT
FULL DETAILS FROM THE FEDERATION OF MASTER BUILDERS
LONDON REGION, 33 JOHN STREET, WC1N 2BB Telephone: 242 7033

Please see above an advertisement by the Federation of Master Builders for a campaign meeting Against Direct Labour and Nationalisation of the Construction Industry held in April 1978. (32)

The employers were very frightened when building workers showed they could come together and win against them as happened in the 1972 national building workers' strike. They did not want to see us establish large trade-union organised public sector Direct Labour Organisations which could successfully compete and take away what they felt should be their work.

¡The attacks on Southwark's Direct Labour Organisation and our response

They did not like it that we already had shown that we were better than they were in meeting the housing demands of local authorities.

This was evident in 1976 when the Chairperson of Southwark's Housing Committee, Councillor Charles Sawyer, wrote to me to congratulate the DLO on our success. This is an extract from his letter:

"The committee were delighted to hear about the profits made by the housing works division (DLO) over the last two years.

They were pleased to note the increased number of completions of finished work within the contract periods. On behalf of the committee I extend my appreciation and thanks for your contribution to these magnificent achievements demonstrating that direct labour can be successful. I am equally pleased that this should occur at a time when private contractors are knocking direct labour as being inefficient and costly. The above achievements give confidence to all and whilst they continue any reduction in workload is most unlikely." (33)

In contrast to this, one of the attacks against Southwark Building DLO occurred in the *South London Press* in June 1979. At that time, we had over 150 painters employed in the DLO, 30 of whom were working on our inter-war improvement sites. Painting and decorating within these properties were subject to a different "new flat standard", so, this work greatly differed from the usual painting and decorating works. This was because this work was being carried out at the same time as other trades' work and the tenants remaining in their homes. This meant, work was much longer than the normal day-to-day painting and decorating activities.

The press report gave the impression that all 150 council painters were taking a long time to decorate the council's properties when only 30 painters were engaged on this type of work. They even quoted adverse comments from two painting subcontractors in this article, when the truth was the council was finding it difficult to get painters to come and work for the council, because of the high standards required for this work.

In 1978, management attempted to impose what was called a "banded bonus scheme" on over 100 direct labour workers, who were working on what was then our largest conversions site at Grosvenor Terrace in Walworth. Initially our bricklayers on this project had refused to co-operate with this new bonus scheme. Other workers on this site were asking what the union was doing about it, yet they were not prepared to do much themselves when they chose to vote against the stewards' recommendation for industrial action.

The attacks on Southwark's Direct Labour Organisation and our response

Everything was not lost, as the bricklayers continued non-cooperation with management's scheme.

It meant this bonus scheme did not last very long and demonstrated to me that even when you had principled shop stewards, as we did on our sites, it didn't always follow that you could get workers to support all our proposed actions.

Our members took many actions in 1979. One of these was when management decided to bring heating contractors onto the Vauban Estate improvements site to replace work being carried out by our own DLO plumbers.

The threat of strike action was enough for management to reconsider their position. Management finally backed down after plumbers among our own DLO workforce came forward to show they had the skills and qualifications to continue to do this work.

We also saw the threat to replace our electricians by bringing electrician contractors onto the Harold's estate site. This threat ended when the contractors who turned up to do the work found they could not access the properties due to the keys to the flats going missing.

Our members stopped work to join a mass picket held at our major conversions site at Braganza Street in Kennington. This came about after the UCATT regional organiser, Jack Kennedy and I were attacked by a contractor.

We saw action from our painter chargehands when 20 of them on our day-to-day repairs and maintenance section decided to end the practice of using their own cars for travelling from job to job. They felt that this continued cynical pretence of management that they could visit painters every day by using buses had to come to an end. It was impossible to get around all their painters without having to use their own cars. The bus fares payment they received was far outweighed by the costs involved in the use of their cars. (38)

They demanded management must pay them the same as office workers. This was a far more generous payment called the "car mileage allowance".

Management still refused to come to an agreement, so the charge hands went on a work-to-rule. The work-to-rule brought about chaos. Painters did not receive work on time and were not supplied with essential materials to do their jobs. Within two weeks there was victory as management conceded. We later got this paid to all other workers who used their own cars for work purposes.

In 1978, two years before the council was to close its new-build DLO Organisation "Southwark Construction" There were 16 new house building projects being carried out by private sector contractors.

The attacks on Southwark's Direct Labour Organisation and our response

These sites had 1,809 homes under construction with an average of 520 weeks delay in completion times and an overspend by 32% = £8 million by these contractors. (30)

Yet despite this failure of contractors Southwark was still determined to close its own new build DLO Southwark Construction. The fight was then stepped up to save Southwark Construction with a strike by the plasterer subcontractor workers on the Hampton Street site. These strikers were demanding continuation of employment by being transferred to the other Southwark Construction sites after work on their site had been completed.

Our steward's committee voted to support these strikers by calling on the council to employ them directly as Southwark DLO workers. We also attended their picket lines and collected money for those on strike.

Despite the evidence of massive increased cost and inefficiency of contractors the Council still chose to close its new build section, DLO "Southwark Construction."

Pictured above shows workers on strike at Southwark Construction in 1980.

In 1980 we saw off a threat to transfer 26 of our DLO painters off the Arnold Estate site and replace them with subcontractor painters. This threat was lifted after only a day when our painters threatened to go on strike. (40)We also saw workers on the Arnold Estate site go on strike for over a week, because of management's sacking of the stores labourer for not declaring that he had dermatitis at the time when he had applied for the job.

The attacks on Southwark's Direct Labour Organisation and our response

The strike was won after we demonstrated that the labourer, "Tony's" disability should not have been used to discriminate against him, when adjustments to his work, together with use of appropriate protective clothing and barrier cream would prevent any further risk to his health. Our arguments, plus the threat of prolonged strike action was enough to persuade management to back down and he was reinstated. (41)

After the strike, the workers were given a week's strike pay by the union. (37) This was a ten-shilling note together with a letter thanking them for their actions and declaring the strike official. This was the first time these workers had got official recognition after taking industrial action. They celebrated by sticking the letter together with the ten-shilling notes on the canteen wall under a large poster declaring their victory. Prior to compulsory balloting for strike action it was rare that any strike in those years would get official support. So, the celebration was understandable.

But, even today the Joint Working Rule Agreement for the construction industry specifically rules out any form of industrial action taken over workers' disputes, unless the anti-union laws have been followed. (20) (29)

There was a threat of further strike action on the Arnolds Estate because the woman canteen worker was getting less pay than the site labourers. Negotiations resulted in an equal pay agreement.

We achieved 100% direct labour employment on our improvement sites in Bermondsey and Rotherhithe. However, this was not always the situation on some of our numerous smaller conversion sites where management's periodic use of subcontracted labour meant we did not always know when they would be brought onto sites.

After 1981, due to the pressure from our shop stewards. the remaining "Housing Works Division" DLO continued to expand. This was the situation until the end of the rate-capping battles in 1986 and contrasted with most other DLOs which started to decline immediately after the election of Margaret Thatcher in 1979. The main reason for our expansion was the abolition of the Greater London Council and later the Inner London Education Authority, together with the transfer of their properties and their building workers.

This increase in our DLO was despite work being lost from 1978 onwards by our major conversions and improvements sites. Yet, throughout this time we achieved no compulsory redundancies because of internal transfers to other sections of our DLO, and there were hardly any voluntary redundancies.

The attacks on Southwark's Direct Labour Organisation and our response

Workers who chose voluntary redundancy were largely the over-50s. who could get voluntary early retirement based on enhanced pensions and redundancy payments.

Many workers who remained had been used to carrying out large construction works and were quite happy when we could get them transferred to our large void works and major small works divisions of the DLO.

Wider attacks on the trade union and labour movement paved the way for even larger attacks on Building DLOs

After 1981 and up to 1990, Southwark DLO workers hardly took any industrial action over issues concerned with their own terms and conditions of work. This was mainly due to there were being many more progressive Labour councillors prepared to reach agreement with us. However, this did not mean there were no strikes – we took many actions in support of other workers.

In 1982, we held a mass meeting in the North Peckham civic centre to hear from a nurse about the reasons for their hospital workers' strikes. We then voted to have a one-day strike in their support and sent a coach load of our workers to take part in a national demonstration and rally in Hyde Park in London.

Seen above are our members at Hyde Park in central London.

The attacks on Southwark's Direct Labour Organisation and our response

1984 Miners strike

The miners' strike of 1984 was a turning point for all building DLOs, as it was for the whole of the trade union and labour movement in our country. (39) While ultimately the miners lost their strike, we would all have been worse off if they had not taken up the fight. It was a dispute that could have been won were it not for the betrayal of the right-wing trade union and Labour leadership.

The Tory government deliberately engineered the miners' strike. They saw the National Union of Miners (NUM) as the backbone of the labour movement, and rightly so.

The NUM had inflicted defeats on Tory governments in 1972 and 1974, effectively bringing down Edward Heath in the latter case. For a decade, the ruling class made their plans, determined that they would not be defeated a third time.

In 1984, the whole of our Building DLO went on strike on two separate occasions in solidarity with the miners, with substantial numbers of our members taking part in demonstrations. After hearing a Kent miner speak at a mass meeting, we decided to set up a 50p a week levy to buy food that we would then deliver to them.

The miners went back with their heads held high on 3 March 1985, marching back to the collieries behind their banners.

Joint Stewards Committee – Building Workers
London Borough Southwark

COAL NOT DOLE

DECISION OF THE
MASS MEETING
12/06/1984

WE WILL BE ON
STRIKE

THIS WEDNESDAY 27TH JUNE 1984.

IN SOLIDARITY WITH THE MINERS.

Can all members wishing to attend the March be
at Copeland Road Depot at 12pm

Above is a poster advertising one of strikes we held in support of the miners.

FOOD TO THE MINERS' FAMILIES

On Saturday 1st September a £2,200 food convoy left Southwark Town Hall for the Kent Coalfields where miners are fighting for a working class right – the right to keep a job.

The food was paid for by a 50p a week levy which was overwhelmingly voted for by the London Borough of Southwark Building Workers.

The miners are now in a major struggle against a Tory Government which is oppressive to trade unions. The levy will also go towards our own support fund which we may have to use in our own struggle now that Southwark has been rate-capped. The threat to our jobs is now building up month by month, and we may find ourselves fighting the same fight as the miners.

Your shop stewards would like to thank all of you for contributing.

Unloading the food in Kent.

Building Workers Support the Miners

The above is a leaflet given out to our members about the food delivered to the Miners in Kent: Those in the bottom picture are Tony O' Brien, George Amery and Peter Abbot with miners' wives in their food store. (39)

103

Above shows Southwark DLO workers together with our banner on one of the many demonstrations we attended in support of the miners (39)

In 1985, in response to a call for support from workers at the Government Communications Headquarters (GCHQ) in Cheltenham, we held a mass meeting at our Copeland Road depot and voted to stop work for the day. The background to this dispute was that in 1984 civil service staff working at GCHQ were banned from trade union membership. The International Labour Organisation (ILO) condemned the ban, but it was only after a Labour victory in the May 1997 General Election that the ban on trade union membership at GCHQ was lifted and the first of the sacked trade unionists returned to work in September of that year.

The erosion of the "rate support grant", the cuts made in 'new-build capital funding', led to the introduction of 'rate capping'. and then the 'poll tax' which had major implications for DLOs and other council services. The Thatcher Government's public sector spending cuts involved a rate cap on 17 local authorities in 1985.

The attacks on Southwark's Direct Labour Organisation and our response

These were: Basildon, Brent, Camden, GLC, Greenwich, Haringey, ILEA, Islington, Lambeth, Lewisham, Merseyside, Portsmouth, Sheffield, South Yorkshire, Southwark, Thamesdown, Leicester and Hackney.

This was followed by the 1985 rate-capping rebellion – a campaign within English local councils aimed at forcing Thatcher government to withdraw the councils' spending restrictions.

The affected councils were almost all run by the left-wing within the Labour Party. The campaign's tactic was to refuse to set any budget at all for the financial year 1985–86, requiring the Government to intervene directly in providing local services, or to concede. However, all 15 councils which initially refused to set a rate eventually did so, and the campaign failed to change government policy. Powers to restrict council budgets have remained in place ever since.

Southwark Council was strongly opposed to making a rate and together with three other London boroughs and the trade unions a joint public campaign of support was set up. The trade union side played a major part in the campaign and we joined with community groups, and tenants' associations, locally, London-wide and nationally. There were many campaign events and demonstrations and our Southwark Building trade unions were a leading force. I jointly chaired the local authority trade union rank and file organisation: "London Bridge". I also chaired a mass meeting of thousands of Southwark's workers called to support the campaign. John Bryan, a UCATT member, was also a leading figure in opposing rate capping in Southwark.

While the leadership of Southwark Council was determined not to set a rate, there were moderate Labour councillors who were willing to comply. On 16 April, council leader Tony Ritchie use his powers to prevent a meeting going ahead to set a legal rate by adjourning the meeting pending new advice. A further meeting on 24 April was also adjourned, this time because Tony Ritchie had collapsed during the meeting and was taken to hospital. The Council finally met on 26th April, the chamber was invaded by members of tenants' groups and council workers with the result that the meeting broke up and had to be cancelled by the Mayor. Finally, on 30 May, the council voted by 26 to 23 to set a rate at the maximum level allowed. (31)

The attacks on Southwark's Direct Labour Organisation and our response

This rightward political move by most councils in the rate-capping struggles opened major attacks on Southwark DLO and all other DLOs throughout the country. The number of those directly employed in Southwark and nationally had declined directly because of the Labour party's move away from its post-war position of nationalisation of industry to the same agenda of privatisation and attacks on public services that began with the election of Margaret Thatcher in 1979.

Lambeth and Liverpool Councils stood out in the rate-capping struggle, and the District Auditor disqualified and surcharged 81 councillors for the costs of not setting a rate – 32 in Lambeth and 49 in Liverpool.

The costs were £106,103 in Liverpool, and £126,947 in Lambeth. In both cases the amount of surcharge per councillor was over £2,000.

Following her election, Thatcher first brought in drastic changes to trade union laws generally known as the "anti-union laws," most notably the regulation that unions had to hold a ballot among members before calling strikes. This led to both Conservative and Labour Parties' attacks on public spending, an end to new council housing, and the acceleration of privatisation of industries and services previously publicly owned. Tony Blair's "New Labour" government continued these policies when elected in 1997.

In 1986, the next major battle against organised workers begun, when 6,000 newspaper workers at Murdoch's News International (NI) including printers, engineers, electricians, journalists and clerical staff went on strike following a move to the newly built Wapping plant. Management responded by dismissing all of those involved, and while management carried out negotiations, they secretly recruited workers through the electricians' union EETPU. From January 1986 EETPU workers, crossed picket lines, protected by the police, to ensure not a single day's production of the four titles: Sun,' 'The News of the World,' 'The Times' 'The Sunday Times' was lost.

At the time, we sent a message of support to David Payne who was a Southwark Labour councillor. David and many other print workers had been subject to charges levied by the police, who themselves were guilty of serious intimidation, violence and provocations on the picket lines outside the Wapping plant.

The attacks on Southwark's Direct Labour Organisation and our response

In 1986 building workers in dispute with John Laing at a site at Hayes Wharf in Tooley Street Bermondsey asked us to support their picket line. Our Weston Street depot was near the site, so I went and got support from the members there, who agreed to attend this picket line the following day. However, to my dismay only a few turned up. I felt there was an important principle at stake – if workers voted for action then they must carry it out, as they risked a backlash from management due to their lack of unity. I went to tell them they were wrong and had another vote, I made it clear that if they voted to support, all of them would have to walk out of the depot and march down the road to this site. And this they did. I think a very important lesson was learnt.

From 1986 onwards Southwark Council was more compliant with the government's wishes when it started to increase the rundown of the operations of its DLOs. It avoided any major battle with us between 1986 and 1990 as it achieved reduced numbers through voluntary redundancies.

After the defeat of the rate-capping struggle in 1986, councils had also begun to make decisions based on balancing their books. The cuts in government grants and rate capping were softened by creative accounting enabling councils to get by without making compulsory redundancies. The leader of the Council at the time was UCATT member Anne Matthews.

What came later were much larger cuts, the privatisation of services, TUPE transfers and compulsory redundancies. In 1986 we wrote a three-page letter to the then leader of Southwark Council, Tony Ritchie, complaining of the rundown of our conversion and improvement site. (43)

For many years trade union activists had waged a major fight against the employment of casual workers which we called 'the lump.' The slogan that could be seen on many placards in the disputes in those days would be "Kill the lump." But in 1987 UCATT recommended to its national conference that self-employed workers should be allowed to become members. At the time, we held a mass meeting of over 900 DLO workers and voted to send a protest letter to the leadership of our trades unions. We also sent a large delegation of our members to UCATT's national conference in Blackpool to lobby delegates.

The attacks on Southwark's Direct Labour Organisation and our response

See above: our delegation to the UCATT conference lobby in Blackpool.

The EEPTU (the plumbers and electrician's trades union) had an even worse union leadership, which joined with the employers' Electrical Contractors' Association (ECA) to form their own company, ESCA Services Ltd.

Using "714 workers"—cash-in-hand casuals who held PAYE schedules and tax exemption certificates. They were cheap and so much favoured for jobs ahead of unionised workers.

In May 1991, through a joint application by the EETPU and the ECA, a Statutory instrument (Extension of Statute of an Act of Parliament) was granted, the effect of which was to exclude all Joint Industry Board (JIB) operatives from section 54 of the Employment Protection Act. This abolished the right of all JIB employees to stand up against unfair dismissal, and consequently they had no right of access to industrial tribunals. (22)

The attacks on Southwark's Direct Labour Organisation and our response

In 1988, a three-year-old girl fell through an unprotected opening left by a sub-contractor employed to carry out work on the Gloucester Grove estate in Southwark. This little girl happened to be the daughter of one of our Southwark direct labour plumbers, (WY). Miraculously she survived without any long-term disabilities.

At the time, we held a mass meeting at our Copeland Road depot and voted to stop work and hold an immediate march to our building direct labour office in Peckham road.

The picture above shows the protest we held outside our main office.

In 1989, Thatcher's continued attacks on local government included her plans for a "poll tax" on council taxpayers. Hundreds of those who refused to pay the poll tax ended up in court. Many were sent to prison when they refused to compromise and pay the tax.

This tax was met with growing opposition, with the largest anti-poll tax demonstration held in central London on Saturday, 31 March 1990, shortly before the tax was due to come into force in England and Wales. The disorder in London's Trafalgar Square was the worst of hundreds of protests throughout the country. Protesters' claims of provocation and police set-ups meant many of those charged were found not guilty.

The attacks on Southwark's Direct Labour Organisation and our response

The poll tax did much to contribute to the downfall of Margaret Thatcher, who resigned as Prime Minister on 28 November 1990. Soon after the government announced abolition of the tax

While Southwark had always used competitive tendering to decide who would get its major capital building works, in 1987-1988 government legislation forced the introduction of "compulsory competitive tendering" extending this requirement to large amounts of Southwark's services including its day-to-day repairs operations, which were previously exempt.

In 1989, prior to the abolition of the Inner London Education Authority (ILEA) we held a one-day strike in solidarity with the ILEA workers and a coachload of our workers travelled to the head offices of our union UCATT to lobby them for support and then on to a march and rally held in central London.

Again in 1989, We sent two coachloads of workers to the Construction Safety Campaign's lobby of Parliament over the huge increases in site deaths in the construction industry's private sector. This was one of the largest events attended by private and public-sector construction workers for many years.

Above can be seen one of the many mass meetings we would hold in all our depots in the 1980s This one being at Copeland Road.

The attacks on Southwark's Direct Labour Organisation and our response

At this time, we had six major depots, the others were at Weston St, Crown St, Lorrimore Road and Sillwood St. All major decision would be taken by mass meetings of our members.

Each year we sent large numbers of workers from our DLO to lobby the employers and our union's national pay negotiations. These would be held at various places throughout the country, so on some occasions they would involve our members starting out as early as 5am to be in time to lobby both sides in the negotiations. These lobbies were important as large numbers of DLO workers throughout the country turned up to show their solidarity and determination to have decent national pay and conditions.

In late 1989 Southwark Council did away with estate-based caretakers and replaced them with mobile estate housing officers, whose job description included various aspects of our trade work. They were reluctant to do this because they did not have the skills and were already bogged down being far fewer in number than the estate caretakers they had replaced. I wrote to the council pointing out that they were putting at risk the jobs of over 270 qualified professional tradespersons and were in breach of the law. They backed down when we threatened to place an injunction on them.

1990 was the year in which for the first time we had lost a large amount of our major repairs and maintenance work in the council's Bermondsey and Rotherhithe area. A company named Beazer (later to become part of Kier Ltd.) won a 12-month contract for all this work and it led to much hardship with up to 150 building trades workers' jobs lost through voluntary redundancy. Yet all this could have been avoided if the council officers responsible for the contract had carried out a proper appraisal of the tender documents.

The real intent of Beazer's was later revealed when it emerged, they had raided Southwark's finances. The actual outturn of their average price for a maintenance repair was proven and revealed at a council committee meeting to be 33% higher than the same work carried out by the council's own Building DLO.

Fundamentally, the business of contractors is to screw as much money out of their clients as possible. You would have thought that the council should have learned a major lesson from this and many other episodes of fraudulent tendering. Sadly, they did not and instead continue their slavish co-operation with the Tories and the running down of our DLO.

The attacks on Southwark's Direct Labour Organisation and our response

The same year saw the departure of Ben Farmer, the head manager for the Housing Works Division DLO since 1970; I had had meetings with him as the DLO trade union convenor for 15 years.

(I had soon learnt it was a waste of my time trying to contact some managers after 1 pm as they were either hard to get hold of, or a bit the worse for wear. Most managers in the 1970s had a cushy number, with the bar at the Liberal Club on Peckham High Street a favourite venue).

However, Mr. Farmer was an old-school type manager; he soon learnt that I was determined to get results for my members and so, while not wanting to give anything away, in general he satisfactorily resolved many issues within his remit.

Any major issues involving pay went to the Joint Works Committee (JWC) our local dispute's machinery, and If no agreement was reached there the issue would be brought before our Joint Consultative Committee of Councillors and Building Workers the (JCC BW). Most of the time during Mr. Farmer's management of our DLO we had a relatively successful disputes machinery.

In 1990, following the end of the Beazer contract fiasco we saw our first management consultant. Mr Sainsbury replaced Mr Farmer as manager and he was followed shortly after by the notorious Mr Keith Fernett who was also engaged as a management consultant, deliberately brought in to substantially reduce our workforce numbers.

Through a mix of voluntary and compulsory redundancies, 400 jobs were lost, preceded by a management announcement to our negotiating body that we were operating at a loss. They said that on the current market analysis against major contractors' prices, we would not be able to win any repairs and maintenance work due to go out to tender in 1991. This put the DLO under threat of closure with the loss of 900 building worker's' jobs. They said the only way we could survive was to agree cuts to our terms and conditions of employment.

We decided to do our own evaluations to check out management's predictions and find out what contractors were submitting for comparable work in the private sector and other local authorities in London area. Our findings were not too dissimilar to our own management's evaluations. So, we then had a hard decision to make. A very hard decision when we had already lost so many jobs since 1987.

After lengthy negotiations, we decided to recommend two main steps to a mass meeting of members: 1) That three days of our local holiday leave be suspended until our trading account showed a profit.

The attacks on Southwark's Direct Labour Organisation and our response

2) That payment due to us of a profit share made from our trading account in 1987-1989 be suspended until the DLO had made a 5% rate of profit on the years following 1990. The condition we imposed was that all officers including senior management levels of the DLO must be part of this agreement (because as they would benefit from the saving of jobs also, then they must be prepared to make the same sacrifices). Management agreed to our proposed conditions. We put this to a vote at a mass meeting and it was agreed without any opposition.

In 1991, tenders submitted from contractors showed that had we not made these compromises our DLO would have lost all the work and been forced to close. However, contractors' low tenders meant we still suffered a loss of about one-third of our work. This brought us into a major conflict with the Council. There were 170 proposed job cuts from a workforce of 850. One hundred were voluntary and 70 were compulsory redundancies. In addition, management proposed to make cuts in some parts of our guaranteed minimum rates of pay these included our minimum bonus payment, sickness payment, bonus targets and flexibility pay. This would mean pay cuts of between £20-£35 per week.

At the time, building DLOs were losing thousands of jobs throughout the country. But we were not prepared to take this without a fight and decided to hold a strike ballot of our members. This was the first-time anti-union laws made us carry out postal ballots to get industrial action from our members. This led to management holding a huge propaganda against us winning these ballots. They produced large posters listing their reasons for our members to vote no in the forthcoming ballot. We responded by issuing our own leaflets and posters.

JOINT SHOP STEWARDS' COMMITTEE - BUILDING WORKERS.
London Borough of Southwark.

DISPUTE NEWS

Building Services

Urgent News 1

Mr K Fernett on behalf of Building Services Management has decided to provide us with Urgent News bulletin item No 1, 2 & 3 with more to come.

The first impression we got when he came to Southwark Council was of a hatchet man, our first impressions have been confirmed.

The following is an answer to lies, misinformation and intimidation, which is contained in these bulletins. You will continue to receive these from Consultants who are given £300-£400 per day to bring in the worst conditions of employment which are practised by the outside Building industry.

What is claimed in these bulletins

1. A strike will prove that we are not interested in service delivery and we will only worsen future job prospects, which could put a further 400 jobs at risk.

Our reply

Our proposal for strike action is taken very seriously by us, the course of action which has been followed by management has meant we have already lost over 250 jobs since last September. Management plans include short term contracts of employment. The only increase in service delivery planned, is by the increased use of subcontractors. Our proposed action is to stop managements threat to our jobs.

Please see above a section from one of our leaflets.

In the campaign for the strike the EETPU, who represented the electricians, did not co-ordinate the timetable of their ballots with the other main unions, TGWU and UCATT. The combined vote of UCATT and the TGWU meant there was only a very small majority for strike action. The EETPU sent no ballot papers to their members prior to a mass meeting held two days before strike action was due to take place. This led to chaos at this meeting. A minority who opposed strike action used it as an excuse to agitate against it. The stewards' committee learned that several electricians had 'phoned the EETPU offices and were told they were to report to work as normal as the EETPU had not given permission for the strike.

The attacks on Southwark's Direct Labour Organisation and our response

Negotiations with Sally Keeble, leader of the council, were scheduled for the first day of the strike. Surprisingly we achieved several concessions, including reinstatement of adult trainee apprentices and employees who had disabilities. Thus allowing us to save about 20 of our members' jobs. It was an achievement to get these concessions prior to us even knowing the outcome of the first day of strike action.

We had decided that, because of the narrow majority vote of UCATT and TGWU members for strike action, we would call a mass meeting on the second day of the strike to find out how many had taken strike action and how many had gone to work. We agreed that if most employees had gone to work on the first day we would hold another vote without any recommendation from the stewards' committee as to whether we should continue the strike. On the first day there was no support and four out of the five repairs and maintenance depots' picket lines reported most had been crossed. The exception was the Frensham Street depot, our largest, with 140 workers where only eight had gone into work, so 94.3% had taken industrial action. This was no surprise to me because most workers at this depot had originated from our improvement sites from the 1970s. These workers had previously been involved in many successful industrial actions and became the strongest supporters of our trade unions.

After hearing my report on the concessions made by Sally Keeble, and the lack of support from fellow workers, the mass meeting voted to call off the strike. This should be seen in the context of workers throughout the country not being prepared to take up the fight in isolation against similar cuts, when the union leaderships were opposed to having a national campaign for strike action to bring down the government. Also, Councils up and down the country had caved in and were carrying out the government's bidding. Without taking on the government there would be no end to the attacks on workers' jobs, pay, and conditions.

This realisation and the outright sabotage by the EEPTU, together with the vicious propaganda campaign led by the highly paid hatchet management consultant Mr Keith Fernett meant our members had no appetite for prolonged strike action.

The attacks on Southwark's Direct Labour Organisation and our response

After the mass meeting, myself and George Amery, who was deputy convenor, had to carry out the unenviable task of reporting the decision of the mass meeting to senior management. We decided to put a brave face on it. Knowing the smarmy head manager, Mr Keith Fernett, would be gloating, we decided to go in with our heads held high. We requested written confirmation of Sally Keeble's agreement of reinstatement of the adult trainees and disabled workers. When Fernett avoided giving us a direct answer we insisted on a proper response. Upon which, he lost his temper and demanded several times that we leave his office. On the fourth occasion, he said "If you don't leave, I will have you removed".

George Amery turned to me and said: "Tony, I wonder who in this room is going to remove us?" At that moment, I looked around the room at four senior managers and noticed they were all looking down at the floor. I looked back at George and we both burst out laughing. Fernett had "egg on his face", as at that crucial moment his managers were not prepared to back him up by risking taking on me and George. No wonder, as George was known to be a body-building fitness devotee in his spare time.

The subsequent return to work was not easy, with one worker, John O' Sullivan deciding to continue a protest over being made redundant by picketing outside the head offices of the building department at Pelican House in Peckham Road. John had the full support of the stewards' committee for his actions.

The attacks on Southwark's Direct Labour Organisation and our response

---

JOINT SHOP STEWARDS' COMMITTEE-BUILDING WORKERS
London Borough of Southwark

GUILTY OF UNFAIR DISMISSAL

So say's the industrial tribunal which was concluded last Monday 11th May 1992.

Remember the first compulsory redundancies!

Inflicted by the (Hachette Man) MR K Fernett when 70 of our workmates was made? compulsory redundant over the Easter bank holiday in 1991.

Your shop steward's committee said then that we would use every single means necessary to seek justice against the outrages attacks on our jobs.

We did strongly advice that all of who was dismissed should make applications to the industrial tribunal. As a result, 22 members did take our advice and after a month of hearings into each separate case the tribunal has found Southwark Council guilty of unfair dismissal. (The other 48 that was mad redundant should have also taken our advice)

We understand that this victory of the Industrial tribunal decisions is the biggest in recent local authority history, we hope that other D.L.O, s who are suffering from the same attacks will take heart from this decision.

We warn all our members.
Although this is good news to see that the industrial tribunal ruled in our favour, management have done damage and will continue to do so unless we show a maximum unity in whatever action we decide in order to defend ourselves in the coming months.

We warned 2 years ago, and we warn now, the more we accept without a fight the impositions of management the more rapidly will management attack our jobs and conditions of employment.

The result of the tribunals meant:
- Over £55.000 in compensation has been awarded (the compensation was based on making up wages to a year's pay from the date of redundancy)
- Five of our workmates have been re-instated. (We could have had the majority re-instated if it was not for a Plea made by the Council that the D.L.O could not be financially viable if the reinstatements did continue."

In 1992 an industrial tribunal ruled on our claim of unfair dismissal for members made redundant in 1991. The tribunal ruled that: "In a rush to make these 70 compulsory redundancies Southwark breached these workers' employment rights.". At the time, we put out a notice to our members which can be seen above. (42)

117

The attacks on Southwark's Direct Labour Organisation and our response

1992, saw the closure of the major roads section of the Highways Division DLO with nearly 200 job losses when the council decided that all future major road works would be carried out by external contractors. What remained was a very small section of 20 workers who were involved in minor works to pavements and street lighting.

In 1993, despite resistance from our shop stewards, management for the first time was able to introduce tender-led schemes into our DLO. Management did this by going behind our backs and holding a secret meeting with one of the sections of our DLO. They successfully enticed these workers with enhanced productivity rates so they would agree to a supposed trial of a tender-led scheme which eventually ended up in full operation. These enhanced rates (predictably) were later withdrawn.

We had opposed these schemes because it tied our productivity to compulsive competitive-tendering prices. It also increased the divisive competition that arose from allowing unlimited earnings. You had a perverse situation in which some workers could earn 300% more than a worker on the guaranteed minimum level of pay. It was sadly no surprise to us that the top earner from this scheme had a serious accident which forced him to retire from work.

In 1993, the contractor Tripps became the second largest contractor when they won four neighbourhoods. They took on a worker transferred under the "Transfer of Undertakings the Protection of Employment regulations" (TUPE) but refused to pay him the same terms and conditions he previously enjoyed while working for Southwark. Tripps subsequently were found guilty of being in breach of the TUPE regulations and were forced to pay out over £30,000 in compensation.

In 1993, we halted what was an increasing trend from 1990 for the council to get non-qualified workers to carry out our jobs. This would become a serious threat to the survival of our DLO. We got UCATT to agree to seek an injunction to prevent this from happening. The outcome from our threat to go to court was enough to get the council to back down. While we continued to have problems over this, they were minor compared with the problems we had in 1990 and 1993.

In 1993, management begun to introduce what they called "counselling" that is, capability interviews. This seemed to us a follow-up to the redundancies and were further attempts to run down our DLO.

The attacks on Southwark's Direct Labour Organisation and our response

The difference between redundancies and capability procedures was that anyone could be sacked if it could be proved they were not capable of doing the job. At least you got redundancy pay if you lost your job due to lack of work. With a capability assessment you could lose your job and get nothing.

The shop stewards' committee asked me to attend these meetings and act to stop management from making any decisions. I was putting myself at risk, but I agreed. The stewards recognised this and said they would give me full backing should I face a backlash over the use of our tactics. The result was that we forced management to agree a rigorous set of criteria which had to be met before they could carry out any capability dismissals. The agreement meant we succeeded over many years in preventing most of our members being dismissed due to such an assessment.

In February 1994, the council decided to close our woodworking joinery workshop. We put in a lot of effort to persuade the council not to close this important element of our DLO. Their decision not to listen prevented our carpenter-joiner and painter apprentices from being trained in the manufacture of various types of joinery and decoration. This also meant all future purpose made-to-fit joinery items could only be supplied by private sector contractors, with the potential of collusion between the joinery manufacturing companies. The council, particularly in the earlier years were more supportive of direct labour, yet after 1986, with very few exceptions they were cowards, having no backbone to resist the dictates of both Tory and Labour governments' pressures to privatise public services.

In 1994, our members held a three-week boycott of work on the Heygate Estate. This followed from actions already taken by the council's lift engineers who discovered the up and down movement of the lifts had caused damaged asbestos-lined water tanks to spread asbestos dust into the loft and lift shaft areas. After we found out we decided to join the lift engineers in refusing to work on the estate until we were fully protected from any exposure. This led to tenants demanding that the council act after they learned that as well as the water tanks being lined with asbestos, their flats also contained the poisonous substance.

A campaign for the safe removal of this asbestos begun to take shape when tenants on the estate called a meeting and asked myself and Alan Dalton to speak at it.

The attacks on Southwark's Direct Labour Organisation and our response

Alan was the best person they could have invited as he was a well-known expert and campaigner on asbestos and environmental protection issues. After our meeting tenants placed posters in their windows protesting the lack of action by the council to protect them.

I was phoned up by an angry housing manager from the Walworth area housing office who complained about my involvement at the tenants meeting. This manager accused me of stirring up trouble for the council in the meeting. Ironically, I believe that management's anger against me led to their attempt to make me redundant the following year.

The asbestos campaigning work on the Heygate began to achieve results when emergency work began on getting the damaged asbestos removed from the water tanks and the flats were made safe. The tenants' actions on the Heygate estate led to many other tenants' organisations in Southwark demanding they be protected from the asbestos that was also on their estates. This led to us having several meetings with management and Southwark councillors. Finally, we met with the leader of the council, John Fraser, who eventually agreed several million pounds would be allocated to begin a survey of all the council's properties for asbestos, this was followed by a programme for its safe removal from the worst affected estates. The following years saw the council hugely scale back on its original commitment towards asbestos removal. I view that decision as crime against the tenants and building workers who would continue to be exposed to this deadly dust.

Prior to this when the GLC and ILEA were abolished a major scandal existed when an asbestos survey of their schools and the housing properties was disregarded and possibly dumped. This survey would have cost millions of pounds to carry out. I feel that this was, yet another wreck less action that was carried out against workers, tenants and a waste of taxpayer's money.

In October 1994. I wrote to the chair of our JCC Building Workers, Councillor Ritchie, over concerns that management was beginning to replace DLO capital sites officers with officers on short-term contracts. I said:

"That this was being done while at the same time some senior managers were attempting to negotiate for themselves short term contracts at greatly enhanced salaries. There are only two directly employed site agents out of seven employed on our capital works sites. These two long standing site agents had now been given notice of dismissal because of their refusal to sign to be put-on short-term contracts. This when they had been employed by Southwark for over twenty years.

The attacks on Southwark's Direct Labour Organisation and our response

Action had to be taken to stop this run down of our Capital works DLO as if not management will have been allowed to have done away with this direct labour organisation and the council would be left at the mercy of a monopoly of sub-contractors. Therefore, we would ask that immediate action is taken, at least the status quo should be carried out"

Despite our repeated warnings the council refused to act. We were proven correct when the district auditor was not prepared to accept the inclusion of the DLO capital sites trading account in the other DLO's accounts.

He said: *"we were not employing sufficient numbers of a direct labour workforce to claim to be a DLO"*, under the accountancy rules for operating DLOs.

The attacks on Southwark's Direct Labour Organisation and our response

SAY NO TO EXTERNALISATION (PRIVATISATION)
OF SOUTHWARK DIRECT

The report before you tonight are designed to convince members that privatization is good for Southwark services. It is full of inaccurate and distorted information and therefore must be totally opposed.

Instead, we ask that management be instructed to reach agreement with the Trades unions to promote the expansion of Direct Labour. If management refuse, serious consideration should be given as to whether these managers are dedicated enough to continue to be employed by Southwark Council.

You must ask yourself? Why is it that the Grammar report opposed all options other than the continuation of DLO's and yet management still seeks privatization?

CONTRACTORS

Collusion and price fixing between contractors will be rampant if the DLO no longer exists. Contractors who have done repairs and maintenance work for Southwark over the last five Years has been diabolical. You must recognize this fact.

Contractors will subcontract the work; subcontractors will engage workers on the lump or under 714s or tax exemption certificates. Tenant's aspirations for neighborhood working with regular contact with those who carry out the work will disappear.

Contractors will be based outside of Southwark. Income will be lost from the Southwark area thus; Council tax will particularly be hit as most of Council workers live in the Southwark area.

DIRECT LABOUR

Southwark maintains direct control and can take immediate actions as it requires. This is not so with contractors. It can provide training, local jobs, equal opportunities and accountability. **We** are already a quality assured organization.

DON'T ALLOW FOR THE BUILDING DLO TO LOSE WORK
BASED ON UNFAIR SELECTION CRITERIA

Safety, Pensions, Quality, and Previous track record allows for Southwark to rule out contractor's tenders that are tested and fail. Managements boycott of the Trades Unions from involvement in risk assessment must be lifted."

The history of Southward's DLO's has been one of unfair bias competition which has resulted in over 2000 lost jobs over the last five years. We ask you to stop this discrimination.

We do not support the interpretation of Management view of the two-stage tendering process. That, the in-house bid will completely fail if it is not the cheapest tender.

There are no guarantees at all for those who may be transferred if externalization was agreed by Southwark. Under threat would be, wages, holidays and Pensions.

In 1995, despite all the evidence we submitted that our work should be kept in-house, we saw the Housing Repairs and Maintenance contract put up for tender. Please see the above leaflet that was handed out to councillors at the time.

122

The attacks on Southwark's Direct Labour Organisation and our response

In June 1995, Southwark's Housing Committee decided that out of its 20 repairs and maintenance contracts, it would award 12 to the DLO, four to Botes, three to Tripp and one to Salisbury. Following this, management decided to cut our wage agreements and transfer 57 of our members to contractors Botes and Tripp under the TUPE regulations. We held an internal ballot of our members in which 79% voted to call on our unions to ballot for industrial action whilst we continued to negotiate with management.

Management threatened to 1. cut tender-led scheme productivity prices by up to 30%. 2. Make cuts to our holiday pay. 3. Introduce a disputed TUPE criteria.

We threatened legal action on behalf of the original 57 workers chosen for transfer. This threat enabled us to get a blatantly discriminatory selection criterion removed which originally said: "a person would only have to have previously worked in a TUPE contract areas to that of: "had previously worked on a TUPE contract area for over 50% of their time". We went on to argue that the DLO had enough work to keep everyone employed if they removed all the sub-contractors carrying out our work. This meant we got those selected for transfer reduced from 57 to six workers.

I was included on the list for TUPE transfers. While criteria for selection of those to be transferred existed, no such criteria were in place for me as the Convenor. Everyone knew I had not spent more than 50% of my time on any of the contract areas, as I was engaged full time on trade union duties. Management followed this up by saying "Full time union release would be done away with from 1st September 1995 irrespective." They were blatantly attempting to break the strength of trade union-organised resistance, and at a time when all our strength was needed.

While they were trying to make me redundant, they were also acting to do away with the senior level of our trade unions negotiation machinery: the "Building Joint Consultative Committee."

John Jones was a bricklayer shop steward on the DLO and was one of the six selected for transfer to Botes. Jones was adamant that he would not transfer as Botes had not yet signed up to provide all the contractual terms of our DLO required by TUPE.

We handed in a petition to Southwark Councillors signed by all our members which deplored management's actions. A meeting of the Housing committee was held that instructed management to draw up a statement agreed by the trades unions that would include within it every part of Southwark DLO workers' existing contractual terms and conditions of employment.

123

The attacks on Southwark's Direct Labour Organisation and our response

This committee further added that these contractors would not be allowed to start any work in the contract areas they had won until they had signed up to every part included within this statement.

At a further meeting, we got management to back down on their proposed cuts to our wages and I was withdrawn from the TUPE list for transfers. Management then gave me a three-month notice of redundancy. The trade union organisers decided not to hold a ballot for industrial action because they felt the council would apply for an injunction because management had conceded "at that stage" to the bulk of the reasons given for the proposed ballot.

My redundancy notice was discrimination, but the three-month notice allowed me some time to combat it, and I was successful in having it removed. The shop stewards' committee had disagreed with the union over the ballot being called off but had accepted that because of the concessions made by management the unions had very little option.

A mass meeting was held subsequently which agreed with the shop stewards' position. John Jones went on to oppose the recommendations of the stewards' committee and the decision of this mass meeting. At the end of the mass meeting I called together the five workers who were due to be transferred over to Botes and Tripp and asked if they would accept the vote of the mass meeting and transfer to Botes. Three workers voted to accept, and transfer, John Jones and Terry Mason refused. Jones then gave notice that he and Terry Mason would instead picket our main depot at Frensham St.

We disagreed with John Jones and Terry Mason over their refusal to transfer to Botes as we knew from legal advice that to refuse meant dismissal from their jobs. We felt we could not go along with what we regarded as a no-win, self-destruct position. Putting a picket on our Frensham Street depot would be seen by our members as a hostile act against them, particularly when a previous mass meeting had already decided the issue.

We were not however opposed to actions of protest to Southwark Council over their use of TUPE and Compulsory Competitive Tendering to run down the DLO. Indeed, we had already carried out several actions including lobbies of councillors and a sit-in at our Frensham Street depot over this. So, we proposed to John Jones and Terry Mason: if they were adamant about refusing to transfer to Botes we had no doubt they would be out of a job. And if this was the case; we would be prepared to pay them their previous full wage if they agreed that they would protest only under the direction of the stewards' committee.

The attacks on Southwark's Direct Labour Organisation and our response

They refused and instead called for a picket of the Frensham Street Depot that involved many others who did not work for the council and were not part of our DLO workforce. I soon realised that they were involved, with John Jones, in a group called the "Building Workers Group" (BWG) which had no interest in protecting workers. Their campaign was personal and directed against me using leaflets and pamphlets calling for my removal as convenor. There were court actions that led to the UCATT Regional Organiser Dominic Heir paying approximately £10,000 in court costs due to his withdrawal from libel actions against the leader of the BWG, Brian Higgins.

My suspicions about the involvement of hostile persons proved correct when some years later Mark Metcalf, who was a close associate of Brian Higgins and his Building Worker Group openly announced in his article in the "Big Issue" magazine, that a police spy named Mark Jenner had been closely associated with himself, Brian Higgins and his BWG. Mark Metcalf wrote that Mark Jenner posed as a building worker between 1995 and 2000. He, together with Mark Metcalf, attended regular pickets over a four-week period outside Southwark Building DLO's Frensham Street depot in support of John Jones and Terry Mason over their opposition to being TUPE transferred to the contractor Botes Ltd. Brian Higgins went on to form the "Defend Brian Higgins" campaign when Dominic Heir the UCATT Regional Organiser threatened him with libel because of defamatory leaflets about what was happening in Southwark DLO.

The campaign secretary of "Defend Brian Higgins Campaign" turned out to be the police spy Mark Jenner who, according to Metcalf, had opportunities to collect information on trade unionists corresponding with the campaign. The extent of this was confirmed later in 2019 when the internal police investigation into black-listing "The Creedon Report" was disclosed to lawyers representing the Blacklist Support Group; it revealed that Mark Jenner had gathered intelligence on "over 300 individuals. (66)

What we had said at the time was proved to be totally correct: Jones, Higgins and their group were adventurist and grossly irresponsible. It therefore came as no surprise to me that later one of this group's leaflets denigrating me was found on the file kept about me by the blacklisting "Consulting Association" organisation. Unfortunately, by the time we found out the police spy Mark Jenner was involved with the BWG, Dominic Heir had already retired from the union in bad health and has since died. What a difference it could have made if we had possessed that evidence years earlier at the time of Dominic's court action. This could have led to quite a different outcome.

The attacks on Southwark's Direct Labour Organisation and our response

The government was forced to set up the "Pitchford enquiry" in 2014 to consider the conduct of undercover police who infiltrated environmental organisations, animal rights groups, anti-racist campaigns, trade unions and left-wing political parties. The hearing held on 27 July 2017 revealed for the first time that undercover police used fake identities to spy on these organisations and since 1968 infiltrated more than 1,000 of them, using at least 144 police officers to do so. Mark Jenner was named as one of the police spies.

In 1998, Southwark put forward a new pay scheme, called the Haye Scheme, for all its officer employers, its manual employees and those employed in the Highways DLO of the council. Central management pulled back from implementing this scheme for the craft workers in our building DLO as they did not relish having to face joint strike action from a united council-wide workforce. UNISON took industrial action, which we supported by instructing our members not to cover their work. While we did not take strike action, this did not stop us from calling on all our members to lobby the council against management's proposals. We also sat on the disputes negotiating committee and played a leading role in getting key concessions from the council. The main concession was a three-year freeze to any job evaluation cuts in pay. The council then introduced the new scheme which is still in operation today.

JOINT SHOP STEWARDS' COMMITTEE-BUILDING WORKERS
London Borough of Southwark

THE COUNCIL IMPOSES SERVANT CONTRACTS!
FULL SUPPORT TO UNISON STRIKERS

You will be aware the Southwark Council have sent out new contracts of employment for Officers and Manual Workers in all departments of the Council. Management threaten the sack if the signature of employees to these contracts are not given by 1st April 1999.

No such letters have yet been sent to any of our Craft members, Drivers or labourers. That is the reason why we are not at this point in time taking strike action. UNISON has taken the decision to give exemption to unison manual workers from taking strike action in CCT areas within Southwark direct.

We are fully aware that should the Officers and manual workers fail to win this dispute with Southwark then we will be under the same attack.

That is why we fully support the reasons for UNISON members strike action. Although we are not yet on strike ourselfs we urge you to support this dispute in any other way possible.

- ## DO NOT COVER FOR OFFICERS WORK WHEN THEY ARE TAKING ACTION.

- ## MAKE YOUR OBJECTIONS KNOWN TO SOUTHWARK COUNCILLORS.

WHAT ARE THESE CHANGES?
- A move away from National terms and conditions with forced implementation of the HAY pay scheme with a cut of up to 30% in pay over the next 5 years for many employees.
- Employees who are redeployed face probationary periods that can see them being sacked without any appeal rights to the Council.
- Removal of contractual employment rights concerning reorganisation, redeployment, and severance payments.
- Even before the contract begins the contract gives notice of the possibility of termination of contract.
- Normal days work can include Saturday and Sunday.
- Implementation of national pay rises subject to local decision on payment.
- No mention of local agreements.
- All terms and conditions are subject to amendment and variation without any reference to local collective bargaining and agreement with the trades unions.

Your shop stewards committee will continue to work closely with the council wide trades unions and do all we can to support them against this imposition.

Above is a copy of the leaflet we gave out at the time.

The attacks on Southwark's Direct Labour Organisation and our response

In 1999. Major voids contracts were taken from Botes and awarded to Fairhurst Ward and Abbot Ltd (FWA). This company agreed to accept Southwark's TUPE conditions, then one week prior to the contract refused to accept that these conditions applied. Southwark Management still went ahead and handed them the work. This led to nine workers, originally TUPE-transferred from Southwark Council to Botes. losing their jobs. UCATT solicitors took this issue through the courts right up to the House of Lords, which decided in November 2004 to refuse FWA an appeal. They had to pay out over £150,000 in compensation.

In 2000, within a year of the council giving out the Housing Repairs and Maintenance contracts, Sainsburys, who had won one of our contracts was removed. The contractor Botes refused to accept the transfer of a council painter but were later forced by an industrial tribunal to do so. They refused to pay an electrician the rate of pay he was entitled to under the TUPE regulations and later had to pay a substantial sum of money to him in compensation.

On 25 September 2003 we balloted for industrial action over management's proposed cuts of between 7%-30% in our productivity prices. The result of the UCATT vote was: 91% in favour of strike action and 97% in favour of actions short of strike action. Management then began to make concessions which they put to the incoming consultant managers of the company named Pinnacle which the council had brought in to run the DLO. The head manager, Mr McCarthy then backed down and agreed to pay the 52 revised codes we had agreed in negotiations.

In 2003 management consultants Pinnacle were brought into our DLO by Southwark Council. They went about dividing work into two main areas. They enforced these changes without reaching any agreement with us. This led to a protracted dispute with them over differences in pay levels. Finally, in 2004 this dispute was resolved by a contingency payment being agreed for those affected by these changes after we made threats to take industrial action.

In February 2005, due to sustained lack of work, we asked management to consider that all craft employees of the building DLO who earned less than £600 per week should receive the £10 per day contingency payment. Management refused.

In March 2006, our DLO building workers as well as many other Southwark Council Workers joined a national strike of over one million local government workers opposed to the government's plans to reduce our pension' schemes.

The attacks on Southwark's Direct Labour Organisation and our response

At the time, we wrote a letter to Alan Ritchie, then General Secretary of UCATT. We requested that a national meeting of all local authority Building DLO stewards be held in order to expand on this strike action, and to take the action prior to the local government elections due to take place so that it would have a greater impact. There was no response from Ritchie.

In December 2006, because of management's plans to hand over our work to Kier and Morrison we decided to launch a huge campaign to reverse this decision. Our strategy was to circulate the well-researched information we had found on these companies to everyone who would listen to our case for retention of our DLO. We knew we had to win the arguments and so that is what we aimed to do by sending it to the tenants, Southwark politicians and the management of the Council.

We got overwhelming support from the Southwark Group of Tenants Organisations and its affiliated tenants' groups. We got good coverage in the local press and held a mass lobby of the council committee due to decide on management's recommendations. Our plans to lobby the council committee must have been leaked to the council officers as they cancelled the meeting and rearranged it for midday on a date in the following week.

This did not deter us when the whole of the workforce stopped work to lobby the meeting. We also sent a rebuttal letter to all Southwark Councillors over the false information sent to them by the contractors and council officers. Because of our intense campaigning, we achieved a partial victory as our DLO was maintained without any compulsory redundancies. The amount of work awarded was slightly less than we had had previously, but overall, we had won a victory.

Our courageous fight was vindicated when we discovered in 2009 that Kier were part of the blacklisting organisation the "Consultative Association" which was involved in the despicable practice of blacklisting construction workers. In 2016 they had to pay millions in compensation as part of the settlement for claims made against them and other contractors by UCATT and other trade unions.

The attacks on Southwark's Direct Labour Organisation and our response

Some of our members can be seen in the above photos both inside and outside the Town Hall in December 20016 when the decision was made to maintain our DLO.

The attacks on Southwark's Direct Labour Organisation and our response

In September 2009, the Office of Fair Trading (OFT) gave Kier the largest fine of any construction company (£17,894,438) for illegally bid-rigging construction contracts.

The struggle continues over the Council giving work to these corrupt contractors. In 2016, despite our protests, the council awarded to Kier what should have been the DLO's work, the contract for repairs for municipal (non-housing) buildings.

In June 2007, Pinnacle management began to phase in the introduction of Opti-time. This is a software computer planning programme which was supposed to deliver more efficient work practices. Instead the use of this computer-generated work planner was having adverse effects on our members' pay and stress levels. Management later compounded this by attempts to introduce the use of hand-held technology. These systems of work gave management total control over when and how work was carried out and imposed numerous unpaid extra work on our members. Despite our objections management continued to Introduce this new system of work.

In October 2007, the main operations manager, Mark Warren, held an early morning meeting of all emergency workers on what he called an 'information meeting' on the work operations system named "Impact Response." I was not going to allow this manager to have a meeting on his own with these workers. I decided to go along, anticipating that he would try to bar me from the meeting.

Prior to the meeting I spoke to the workers involved to make sure that should he attempt to prevent me from being there they would walk out. I proved to be correct as immediately Warren walked in he told me I had not been invited, as it was a management meeting. I said that these matters involved industrial relations and refused to leave. Warren replied that I could stay but only as an observer as this was a briefing meeting therefore questions were not required.

However, Mark Warren did not get his way; the emergency workers held their own meeting with me and then called him back into our meeting to tell him they had decided that no trial period of the proposed devices would take place without an agreement first being reached with the trade unions. Many meetings followed over the years in an attempt by us to reach agreement over the use of this equipment.

The attacks on Southwark's Direct Labour Organisation and our response

2007-2008 was the worst period we ever experienced under a leading operational manager. We had to take our disagreements all the way to the top of our dispute's procedure. It was then that the DLO contracts, which had already been extended twice up to September 2008, were due to be decided upon by the Executive Committee of the council. So, we faced a dilemma. We did not want to be in a position of serious disagreement at corporate level at the same time as these managers would also be deciding on our future work. So, we decided to suspend our failure to agree at this level.

One of the other main problems we had in 2007-2008 was over Pinnacle management making deductions from our members pay. By October 2008, management had for the first time attempted to make the emergency workers (and later other workers) fully operate the mobile phone hand-held technology devices with their Impact Response system. There followed an initial resistance to changes from these workers, this finally ended in a chaotic introduction of this new system with all our warnings about the effect on pay being realised. Over the next two years management would make some changes to their systems, but we had a hard battle with them over trying to get any payment for all the extra work necessitated by this new apparatus.

In July 2009, management attempted changes to our home parking agreement that would severely put limitations on its use and increase our costs. Fortunately for us, we were all very much aware of our long history of use of the vehicles in our DLO. After management got our response, they soon gave up the ghost.

In late 2009, management negotiated a revision to prices from the housing department for jobs done. This was the first time that they completely realigned job ticket prices with that of productivity pay price. Management deliberately excluded us from these negotiations and then lied when they claimed there would be no cuts in our prices because of this exercise. This was done by changing the price codes that involved less work to ones that involved a lot more work. They were called SOD and SOR codes. For the plasterers, this was a major cut to their productivity pay. There was a prolonged struggle, and we were successful in negotiating an agreement to resolve the plasterers' dispute.

However, management reneged on this agreement which (in July 2011) led to the plasterers successfully taking their case to an industrial tribunal. Even after we won the tribunal, management tried to delay reaching an agreement with us over payments owed.

The attacks on Southwark's Direct Labour Organisation and our response

In January 2010, we held a meeting with the senior housing repairs manager, Mr D Hollas to resolve the dispute. We put forward our own proposals for a salary wage. Initially Mr Hollas said he was not opposed to this in principle, but he ended by rejecting it.

Management's continuing efforts to drive down pay were starting to have effects when we received information on a drop-in productivity performance pay levels of our members based in the Day-to-Day Repairs and the Voids section of the DLO. We held a mass meeting on 12 November 2010 and voted for industrial action over threats to our jobs and our terms and conditions of employments.

In response to our decision to ballot for industrial action the director of housing Jerry Scott announced:

1. She would not continue with changes to the productivity agreement for the time being.

2. This was because she intended to bring the management of Southwark Building Services (SBS) back in-house as well as restructuring it.

3. David Lewis, her second-in-command would meet us over the issues of the cuts previously made to our productivity rates of pay.

4. The introduction of hand-held technology, scheduled to be fully implemented from 4 April 2011 would now not continue for the time being, because of the restructure of SBS and management's intentions to bring the management of SBS back in-house.

This back-down by management enabled us to withdraw from our planned ballot for industrial action of our members.

In 2010-2011, while our threat of industrial action had removed any forced changes to our agreements, management continued to seek voluntary redundancies and they refused to rectify their manipulations over our productivity rates of pay. We, however, were not going to allow them to make redundancies without a major fight against their use of sub-contractors.

Initially, when we raised the issue of sub-contractors with Gerry Scott, the Director of Housing, we were surprised to receive some support when she ordered her manager, Dave Lewis, to conduct a joint review with us over their use. We then set up teams to consider the feasibility of DLO workers replacing the work done by contractors. Lewis, who previously refused to give us information about the amount of work being carried out by sub-contractor was then obliged to do so.

The attacks on Southwark's Direct Labour Organisation and our response

There was no doubt whatsoever there was a culture of putting our work out to sub-contractors. We knew it was hard to break this culture as it meant officers and management had far less work to carry out with far less responsibility. It was however against Southwark Council's policies and was not in line with Southwark's responsibility to mitigate against job losses which could prevent unnecessary pension and redundancy costs to the council and its taxpayers.

The figures Lewis supplied to us allowed us to follow up on Gerry Scott's offer that we should be considered for this work and any other sub-contracted work deemed to be 'specialist sub-contractors work', as well as the work sub-contractors were doing to allegedly meet the so-called 'peaks and troughs' of our work.

In 2012, the plasterers' dispute over the cuts to their productivity rates of pay continued. We returned to the industrial tribunal and Southwark was ordered to produce a joint indexed account of all information that must be made available to the parties and the chair of the tribunal." This would cause some major problems for us. Our issues were:

1. We needed to show the differences when two persons were on occasions working together.

2. We had to make sure that daily losses were not averaged out to show losses not being set against gains as productivity pay was calculated weekly.

3. We asked our solicitors to consider taking out an injunction against Southwark to prevent them from carrying out any future deductions from pay.

4. This needed to account for the continuing deductions they had made since December 2011. We needed legal advice as to whether we should take out another tribunal claim, or whether we could sue for breach of the tribunal decision.

5. While eventually we got back-dated compensation it was not at the level we were looking for. Neither were we able to go back and get the previously cut codes reinstated as this would have involved taking out another tribunal claim against Southwark.

For many reasons, this was becoming very difficult, mainly because of the enormous amount of paperwork involved. With the onus on us to prove the amounts owed, which was not easy due to management's 2010 decision to stop the call centre from allowing the plasterers to record the productivity codes that management was refusing to pay.

So, unless individual plasterers kept their own records for every bit of work they did. they would not be able to produce the evidence the tribunal required.

Many other factors led to this dispute not going any further. The main one was that several plasterers had taken up the offer of voluntary redundancy, added to this were ongoing attempts at victimisation against the plasterer steward. Those plasterers who remained were understandably worn down by the lies, and bureaucratic procrastination used by management.

Shop Stewards and Joint Negotiation Set-Up on Southwark

The building trades unions had a large representative involvement in the council, both consultative and for negotiations. We aimed to achieve progressive policies with the other non-building unions, whether from taking part in joint protests and industrial actions or being involved in negotiations with senior management.

Our Building DLO negotiations changed over time, were on a much smaller scale, and more difficult to maintain when the council had moved more politically to the right. Listed below are some of the various negotiation and consultation meetings we have been involved:

- Depot monthly meetings, of joint stewards/safety reps with management.

- Joint Works Committee (JWC), monthly meetings between senior stewards and management

- Joint Safety Committee, monthly meetings between senior safety reps and management.

- Joint Corporate Council wide safety committee, three monthly meetings involving all trades unions and department managers.

- Joint Consultative Committee Building Workers (JCC BW) monthly meetings between senior stewards and councillors.

We had at various times been represented on many other council committees, some of these were: The Apprentices Working Party, the Contractors' Sub Committee, the Pensions Committee, and the Disability Working Party. From 1975-2000, any major changes in our terms and conditions of employment had to be ratified by what was called the council's "Establishment Committee". From 1978-1995 we could have written submissions placed before Southwark council committees and were allowed speaking rights at these committees. The council had to negotiate and hold consultations with us before any changes could be made to any of our main terms and conditions of employment.

Shop Stewards and Joint Negotiation Set-Up on Southwark

Later, things changed when most non-council-wide changes could be agreed between the Head of Management of the DLO and our unions without having to be ratified by council committee. Meetings with the DLO management resulted in many changes made to our joint agreements. It was strictly the policy of our joint shop stewards' committee that all major agreements made with management had first to be ratified by the stewards' committee and then finally voted on at a members' mass meeting. There were some occasions when decisions were made by our members from a combination of workplace meetings and workplace ballots.

Work gangs in depots and construction sites elected their shop stewards and trade union safety reps. Their representatives on the various negotiations and consultation meetings with management were decided from the stewards in these locations.

After only being with the council for nine months I was elected convenor for the Council's building workers. This happened because the previous convenor Fred Stansbury retired in March 1976. Upon my election I proposed the stewards' committee adopt a policy of "the right of recall and dismissal of the convenor."

That meant the convenor could at any time be removed from his position if a democratic procedure for removal had taken place beforehand.

After 1991, ballots for industrial action, which were mainly for strike action, were conducted from our trade union's national offices. At various times, many different types of successful actions were taken without a ballot.

In September 1991, the council gave formal recognition to the Electrical and Plumbing Industries Union (EPIU). We supported this because over 70% of the council's plumbers and electricians were EPIU members.

This change came about due to most electricians and plumbers resigning from the Electrical Electronic Telecommunication & Plumbers Union (EETPU), and joining the EPIU. While the shop stewards' committee decided to support this action, it wasn't a decision we took lightly. The background was that the national leadership of the EETPU had publicly stated they would attempt to de-stabilise UCATT by poaching its members. Over the previous 10 years the EEPTU had opposed every major struggle taking place against the employers and the Government. They had openly sided with employers and the Government in the following disputes:

1. The hospital workers' struggles of 1982-83.

2. The miners' strike of 1984-85.

Shop Stewards and Joint Negotiation Set-Up on Southwark

3. The Wapping printers' strike of 1986.

These betrayals and many other examples of the EETPU supporting the employers against other trade unions led to its suspension from the TUC in July 1988.

In 1991, in Southwark, the EETPU had acted deliberately to obstruct us from carrying out strike action. They sent out ballot papers late so the action could not be coordinated with the other trade unions. This left us with no clear idea as to what the combined feelings of our members were over our call for strike action. They wrongly described our dispute on their proposed ballot papers. As a result, EETPU members were confused by the ballot, with only a minority even bothering to vote. The EETPU official held secret meetings with management ahead of the strike ballot and had agreed cuts to our pay. (This lack of cooperation from them damaged our ability to win the disputes.)

In 1995, the council ended our Joint Consultative Committee Building Workers (JCCBW). Shortly after they went on to end the officer and manual JCC negotiating bodies of Southwark. This was probably the most reactionary period of anti-union attacks that we faced from Southwark Council, in stark contrast to the high regard with which the council had recognised and encouraged the involvement of its trade unions in 1974.

The Joint Shop Stewards Committee Support Hardship Fund

After the miners' strike ended in 1985, we held a mass meeting and voted to continue a levy we originally had to support the miners. This was at a reduced rate per week. We knew after the miners' strike, we would be in for a battle with the Thatcher-led government over our jobs, pay and working conditions.

So, we made it clear to our members they would be required to take up the fight in the coming months and years and that our fighting fund would assist us during periods of severe hardship

We also agreed that the hardship fund would be used to help alleviate the distress that many of our members could face if they had long-term sickness and other hardships. The fund was also used to support acts of solidarity with other workers involved in industrial actions and the campaigns that existed over struggles against injustice. The fund allowed us to send delegates to attend conferences, meetings and protests concerned with the issues of our members. Our hardship fund was of enormous benefit as it enabled us to get our members involved in supporting our trades union activities.

Apprentices

Between 1982 and 1992 we had the largest number of building trades' apprentices, up to 150 and in addition we had adult trainee apprentices. Because the role of the apprentice mentors formed such an important part of the apprentices training, they were paid an additional plus rate.

Many apprentices after becoming fully qualified tradespersons would later become shop stewards and safety reps. Apprentices and adult trainees elected their own shop stewards and held monthly joint meetings with management. The council recruited what they called an "apprentice master". This was a full-time position managing the council's apprentices.

At that time, apprentices carried out a full range of work so they could achieve all the skills required for competence in their chosen trade. Until 1980 apprentices were exchanged between the council's housing new-build division, Southwark Construction and our housing Conversions/rehabilitation and Maintenance sections.

After 1980 we continued these exchanges by having six-month placements on Southwark's contractor's new build construction sites. The best opportunities for learning a full range of skills was on the older properties involved with our Conversion/rehabilitation site works.

Our apprentices would, with the support of selected tradespersons, carry out this work from beginning to end on numerous apprentice conversion and rehabilitation projects.

Apprentices

Pictured above is one example of the type of houses that are situated in Nunhead Green area in Southwark that DLO apprentices had worked on in the 1980s.

Each year the council held an "Annual apprentice prize-winning awards ceremony" attended by all apprentices, their parents and friends.

The shop stewards' committee also presented their own awards at these events and on some occasions, combined these with socials with live music: on one occasion featuring apprentices who had formed their own band.

Our fight for Health and Safety

For construction workers, retirement is a Health and Safety issue

In contrast to the government's present trend of raising the retirement age, in the 1970s and early 1980s many Southwark DLO building workers and other DLO workers in local authorities got early enhanced pensions and other payments if they had had a serious accident at work, or could not continue at work due to ill health. Since then the local government pension scheme, with its national and local enhanced benefits has been greatly reduced.

Our DLO construction workers gained hugely from medical retirement benefits, as most of these would have already worked many years in the private sector and suffered from accidents at work. Common injuries were repetitive strain and damage to lungs from building dusts. In addition to the benefits from the national agreement for Local Authority's pension provisions, several local authorities would have their own local enhancements.

In the 1970s, our own local agreement included us in the "Croydon Scheme". This scheme allowed workers who could no longer work because of work-related ill health to retire early and get payments equivalent to their average pay while they had been working. This hugely beneficial retirement pay was made up of state benefits they would have received which were topped up by the council to full pay during retirement. In addition, they could receive an up-front payment for any injuries incurred at work with the council, provided this was considered in any personal injury claim made by their union. This scheme was closely monitored. Those benefiting were examined by the council's doctor every year up to the age of 65 to make sure they continued to be incapable of work and were entitled to these payments.

After 1985, while the scheme still existed, it was harder to obtain all its benefits, as each individual claim had to have with it a report from our DLO management. This report had to show that the DLO could afford these additional local enhanced payments and they would not put the DLO trading account in jeopardy. Despite this difficulty, we succeeded in obtaining these local enhanced retirement benefits for our members in most cases up until the mid-1990s.

The council's "accident and ill health scheme" remained in force between 1995-2010, but government attacks on the Local Authority pension scheme made it much more difficult for us to obtain the benefits.

Our fight for Health and Safety

The government allowed Local Authorities to restrict the length of time for which these early retirement pensions could be paid, by creating three levels of ill-health on which workers had to be assessed. While the terms of the ill health retirement scheme were not as good as before, it remained a major gain, especially if you look at the private sector from which most building workers retire with nothing other than what they themselves may have put aside.

On many occasions, we had the added problem of having to battle with management, who would try to retire workers with the use of the council's capability procedures, instead of the accident and ill health scheme. Yet hardly anything is said about the senior council managers and private sector employers when official statistics show their pensions and salaries to have grown enormously. Hardly anything is said too about private-sector employers who have caused many construction workers to retire into poverty, struggling to cope with injuries suffered during years of working in appallingly unsafe conditions.

Oil-based paints

In the 1980s, we were approached by management who told us that doctors who worked out of the London School of Hygiene and Tropical Medicine had asked if our painters would be examined as part of their research into the effects of oil-based paints. At the time, Southwark employed its maximum number of painters, over 150. We were suspicious of management's motives when they asked us to take part in this research project and decided to check out the validity of this with our union UCATT. UCATT indicated it was acceptable for us to help with this research. Our painter shop stewards were supportive, because they increasingly felt unwell when working with these paints. They hoped that their contribution to this research would lead to alternatives being found to the oil-based paints then in common use.

There were 12 gangs of painters in our DLO. We met with each one of them, together with the research doctor and a nurse to get volunteers. Painters who volunteered would be questioned and examined. One of the main requests made from the painters at these meetings was that they wanted a copy of the outcome of their examination. This was agreed with the doctor who went on to examine over 20 painters. After several months went by without any feedback from this research, we complained to our senior human resources officer.

Our fight for Health and Safety

Following several further complaints, with the help of Alan Dalton (Alan was a friend of ours, as well as being a known specialist in toxic substances and a safety campaigner) we decided to write a letter of complaint to the British Medical Association.

Finally, we got a reply and an apology from the BMA. We later found out that these researchers were also being used by paint manufacturers. For us, this showed the double-standards of some in the medical profession and the extent to which the paint industry was using the medical profession to get evidence in order to retain oil-based paints. Despite the complaints made to management about this research, they were still keen that our painters should continue to use oil-based paints. Management claimed these paints were more reliable in resisting damage caused by condensation within rooms such as toilets, bathrooms and kitchens. They continued to deny there was any serious health hazards from these paints.

All this prompted us to carry out our own enquiries on the effects of oil-based paints on our painters. We then received numerous reports that painters had felt dizzy when working with these paints. One painter gave a stark response when he said: "I knew there was something seriously wrong when, after working with these paints, on a Friday I would come home from work and have lunch, brush my teeth and have a bath, and get dressed in my new clothes before going out for a drink at my local pub." He said, "My mates in the pub would often comment that they could smell paint fumes on my breath while they were chatting to me". Resistance begun to grow when many of our painters decided they had had enough and took direct action by refusing to work with this paint. This eventually led to management finding alternative water-based paints.

While still not banned in the UK, the campaigning work of the Construction Safety Campaign and others about the dangers of oil-based paints has created much more public awareness. Most major building suppliers have been made to find alternatives which are now more commonly sold in most building supply outlets.

Contractors, Contractor Managers and our Health and Safety

Unsafe incidents which have occurred in DLOs, including ours, have always taken place because of pressure from DLO management to adapt to the unsafe practices of the private sector. Overall, the safety record of local authority DLO organisations have proven to be far better than that of the private sector who have over many years caused thousands of deaths, injuries and disease from unsafe events.

142

Our fight for Health and Safety

The difference in our own DLO and many others is that while we did suffer from our own accidents at work, it would have been far worse without the fight we waged against the various contractors and the unsafe methods of work they tried to impose.

From my start at Southwark in 1975 there were a whole number of events that convinced me of the need to join with others to form a national campaign on construction safety. This eventually happened in 1988 after an outcry over the then huge increase in construction site deaths. This led to the formation of the "Construction Safety Campaign."

For me the most disturbing incident was in the mid-1970s which involved the death of a construction worker working for a company contracted to carry out a roofing repair job on a council house just off Peckham Road. It emerged later that the contractor had only provided a roofing ladder and not any scaffolding protection for the work to be carried out.

Immediately I found out about this incident I went down to the house which was occupied by an older female tenant. This tenant told me how she had been standing looking out of her lower ground floor window when this roofing worker had fallen to his death. She said she heard a scream, and, in a flash, she saw him falling to the ground. As she described this to me, she was clearly still very upset and started to cry.

The other incident that affected me occurred in the late 1970s, when one of our DLO painters fell from a ladder. This painter had been working on the windows of an old terraced house near Peckham Rye Park. He was standing on a ladder painting the windows on the first floor of this house when the ladder he was standing on slipped sideways and fell. The ladder was not tied in, and was not footed by another worker, even though there had been an apprentice on site who was carrying out other works. This painter suffered severe head injuries and died after a year as a result of complications. The union won a compensation claim on behalf of his widow. As the union branch secretary, I had the unenviable task of handing this over to her.

Until the mid-1980s contract specifications for major work could include the use of cradles to carry out the work of window replacements and repainting of the exteriors of tower blocks. This resulted in a serious incident which took place at a Galleywall Road Estate. This was an external painting job carried out in 1976. This happened when one of the roof support mechanisms to a cradle had worked loose which resulted in one side of the cradle tipping over.

Our fight for Health and Safety

The painter, who was at the time working from what I remember as the sixth floor or above, was then left clinging to the cradle without being able to lower it to the ground. He had to wait for over half an hour for the Fire Brigade to rescue him. The painter was affected both physical and mentally, and we got him early retirement with compensation and enhanced pensions payments. While we argued against the use of these cradles to carry out this type of work management did not listen and preferred to use the Health and Safety Executive's publicity to claim that these cradles were still safe.

In the early 1980s, we had another incident involving the use of cradles when the management at Coopers Road Estate site insisted it was safe for DLO workers to remove and replace window frames from the platforms of cradles. This was even though our own safety risk assessment showed that this was not a safe way to carry out this work.

We already had the experience of the incident at Galleywall Road and now were faced with this. Added to it were wet and windy conditions in which these cradles were being operated. Management refused to listen to our arguments and made unsuccessful attempts to force our members to carry out this work. Despite the threats of victimisation, our members stood firm and refused.

Long before we got better asbestos protection laws in the UK and before we had forced a change in our national union's policy on asbestos in 1976, health and safety activists were constantly warning our members of the dangers. In contrast, management would always try and cover it up.

For us, it was very difficult to monitor when our members might come across asbestos, when it was not always easy to know what work our members were carrying out at any one time. So much misinformation was circulated by our management, the manufacturers of asbestos products and the media. We therefore did not always find it easy to persuade all our members to refuse to work with it.

In Southwark in the 1970s, there were over 15 gangs of painters who mainly worked on external decorations in the summer months. Behind our backs, management would encourage painters to carry out redecoration of prefabricated properties lined with asbestos. They did this by giving painters enhanced rates of productivity pay for this work.

One day, when I saw a gang of painters carrying out this work, I decided to confront the painter chargehand of this gang and warned him that as a union member he should not be getting his painters to do this unsafe work. Twenty years later, I was shocked when he came to see me.

Our fight for Health and Safety

Previously a well-built stocky man, he now looked frail and severely reduced in weight. I was saddened when he told me he had a diagnosis of asbestos-related mesothelioma and had only around six months to live. When I went to get permission for legal aid from the union to make a claim against Southwark, I was dismayed to be told that he did not qualify because he had not kept up his union dues when he retired from work.

Politicians' increasing devotion to privatisation put a great strain on Direct Labour Organisations' health and safety. Those still managing to operate in the 1990s were being subjected to enormous attacks from "consultant" managers brought in by mainly Labour-controlled councils. One attack took the form of discouraging workers from working together by penalising productivity pay when they insisted on two men working.

This led to Southwark DLO suffering one of our worst unsafe incidents in 1994, when one of our glaziers fell and suffered major injuries to his legs while working from a ladder. We went on to hold a protest against Southwark Council and its management outside the magistrates' court when they were prosecuted by the Health and Safety Executive and found guilty. A struggle also took place to make sure that our member received full and adequate compensation for his injuries.

In January 2003, I wrote a letter of complaint to the manager of the Highways DLO concerning the way a fitter/welder had been treated after severely damaging his shoulder in a serious accident at work. The injury meant he was unable to carry on working in his trade. The incident occurred when he and another worker lifted a heavy generator onto the back of a lorry's high platform, when he should have had the use of a lorry with a mechanical-aided lifting device.

Management responded brutally by attempting to use capability procedures to sack him. This we were not prepared to accept. In the end we got this worker redeployed into a job he was happy to do. After 10 years in the new job he was able to leave Southwark on good terms with a reasonable retirement and pension agreement. He also got substantial damages from the union's claim against Southwark for his serious injuries. This kind of intervention meant numerous building DLO workers came out with satisfactory retirements over the 36 years I worked at Southwark.

I can also list below what I recall of the most serious unsafe incidents from 1975 and 2012 when I was employed in Southwark Building DLO:

1. Workers exposed to damage caused by asbestos in Southwark Council's properties.

Our fight for Health and Safety

2. A bricklayer falling from ladder at roof level from property in Havel Street.

3. A carpenter falling down the stairs of council flats in Walworth while carrying heavy and awkward materials.

4. A labourer falling from scaffolding at our major conversion site at Devon Mansions.

5. Contamination of plumber from bird droppings in loft area of flats in East Dulwich.

6. A Labourer burned from a gas leak explosion at conversion site hut at Peckham Rye Flats.

7. An electrician apprentice burned by electric explosion at flats of intake cupboard in Walworth Road.

8. Head damage to an electrician from unsecured door while gaining access to loft in Peckham Road flats.

9. Carpenters violently attacked by drug users while working in flats on North Peckham Estate.

10. A labourer burned from an explosion from a toilet pan chemical blockage in Walworth Road Estate.

11. Major near-miss unsafe incident of collapsed wall at conversion site at Grosvenor Terrace.

I used these examples to argue for greater accountability in health and safety from our own DLO management towards the workforce. I was successful in getting improvements in the way that the council scrutinised contractors' safety standards, and any who failed to comply were removed from the council's approved lists.

Asbestos

We succeeded in getting an expert asbestos support unit set up in Southwark in the early 1980s after we waged a campaign for it. Thousands of life-saving activities were carried out by safely isolating and removing asbestos from the council's properties. The biggest safety issue for us was always the danger of being contaminated by asbestos.

In 1982, following on from the UCATT national delegate conference decision: to "ban the use of all types of asbestos" we ordered our members to refuse to work with it. Our carpenter stewards with the support of the storemen put locks on the parts of the stores doors that held the materials and refused to allow management the keys. (36)

Our fight for Health and Safety

Because I felt it important to make my members aware of its dangers, I listed the names of all our DLO workers who had died from it on the wall of the union office.

The picture above is of Southwark DLO asbestos-removal workers getting ready to carry out their tasks.

Ever since I started to work with Southwark in 1975, I kept records of all complaints we made about members threatened with exposure to asbestos, and I continuously raised complaints about asbestos on the many joint safety meetings we held with management.

In March 2003, I sent evidence to Councillor Lorraine Zuleta who was then the chairperson of our joint councillor/management, union committee. (This very important evidence is kept on file as well as being summarised in the 1st edition of this book)

In 2004, I wrote to Southwark management to inform them I was diagnosed with having asbestos pleural plaques. Later, I made a successful claim through UCATT's solicitors and received compensation. My brother, who worked as an electrician, was also diagnosed with contamination by asbestos.

There were numerous friends of mine, mainly trade union activists, who were contaminated by asbestos. Some of those developed pleural plaques, pleural thickening, and some had mesothelioma (who had died from it). These included: Denis O'Brien, Bob Gordon, Andy Higgins, Peter Turner, Tommy Finn and many others.

The struggle over asbestos continued until I left Southwark in February 2012, and I have no doubt it will continue in Southwark and throughout the UK until it is completely removed from all buildings.

In February 2003. Southwark Council proposed to close our Asbestos Removal Support Unit. In response, I wrote to the then Strategic Director for Environment and Leisure Department, Gill Davies. Despite my letter and appeals made to the Labour-controlled council, to their shame they went ahead and closed the Unit. Its establishment in the early 1980s had been a real breakthrough.

In 2004, T/S who was a shop steward for the painters had a serious accident when riding his motorbike at work. This meant he had to have one of his legs amputated. We immediately supported him and visited him in Lewisham hospital. We made sure that he was given the unions' legal advice so that he gained compensation. We held a mass meeting to report his situation to members who then agreed to a substantial donation from our "support hardship fund". We were dismayed at the lack of concern from management and requested that someone senior visit him and reassure him that the council would act with the best intentions towards him in the awful situation he was going through.

We also applied for compensation from the council's "Personal Injury Allowance Scheme" and were successful in obtaining substantial compensation payments.

Southwark DLO support for the Construction Safety Campaign

I am proud of the fact our Southwark DLO struggles were always linked to the wider ones of workers. The history of Southwark DLO safety campaign activities was from 1988 very much tied up with the work of the "Construction Safety Campaign" (CSC).

I became the founding Secretary of the Construction Safety Campaign in 1988 and stood down in 2013. In 2010, I published a book to commemorate over twenty years of the history of the campaign.

Southwark DLO support for the Construction Safety Campaign

I have copied here some sections of this book together with a few updates, as I believe these records show that Southwark DLO workers, among many others, made a huge contribution to the successful work of the CSC.

Thatcher's first government's attacks on the trade union movement brought about a huge increase in construction worker deaths without any adequate response taking place from our trades unions.

Despite all obstacles, the most politically aware construction activists in the London area decided that they were not prepared to put up with this. We held two meetings in Parliament with Teresa Shanahan a leading Tower Hamlets councillor, local Labour MP Mildred Gordon and Eric Heffer MP, to discuss the consequences of this serious decline in safety standards.

Eric Heffer was a carpenter by trade and had over many years advocated justice for construction workers. Our meeting agreed that an independent campaign was needed that would involve construction trades union members and anyone who supported the aims of the campaign. The meeting elected its founding officers: Jim Franklin as chair, Tony O'Brien as secretary, and Andy Higgins as treasurer.

When an oil platform in the North Sea off the Scottish mainland, called Piper Alpha, caught fire and exploded in 1988, 167 men lost their lives. Public outcry led to a public inquiry and eventually to new laws and changes to the offshore safety enforcement regime. While in the same year, 151 construction workers were killed, in the previous year (1987) 158 lives were lost in the United Kingdom in separate incidents. There was no public outcry, no public inquiry, and no change to the law. (22)

Many of the fatalities were not even reported in the press. Construction workers felt no one cared about these avoidable deaths.

Southwark DLO support for the Construction Safety Campaign

Site workers demand higher fines for negligence

Site workers from the Construction Safety Campaign outside the Health and Safety Executive's press conference in London, yesterday.

Pictured above is our protest held on 13 May 1988 taken outside offices where the Health and Safety Executive were to announce huge increases in construction deaths and serious injuries.

The last three people shown on the right-hand side of this picture are Southwark DLO shop stewards: Arthur Jolly, George Amery and Trevor Williams.

Each year the Health and Safety Executive held a ritualistic press conference to announce the annual figures for deaths and serious injuries that had taken place the previous year.

We were outraged when we learned from this press conference that there was a national 10-year all-time high with 158 construction worker fatalities occurring in the UK that year. In London, there was a 30-year all-time high with 37 construction workers killed. Yet a mere three per cent of fatalities at work resulted in prosecutions. The average fines in the Crown Court were £2,145. Over 97 per cent of cases went to a Magistrates Court where the average fine was £505 and no one at all was sent to jail.

We publicised the fact that world-wide two million workers died each year from work activities, one death every fifteen seconds, six thousand a day. We publicised the fact that: "Work kills more people than wars, and it injures and mutilates more."

Southwark DLO support for the Construction Safety Campaign

CSC supporters would go to the sites where a death had occurred and stage a peaceful protest with banners and give out leaflets to the workers going into work.

We tried to find out what had occurred and to promote site union organisation. On many occasions, we issued a press release prior to the protest to try to get the media to attend. Sometimes work stopped and a brief meeting was held outside the sites. We attended coroners' courts into deaths of construction workers to find out that the most common court verdict was "accidental death."

Seen here above in 1992 is a picture of the aftermath of the collapse of the St Johns Bridge in Lewisham that claimed the lives of Nicholas Scott and Frank Warren.

The campaign achieved its first unlawful killing verdict at the inquest into the St John's Bridge disaster in South London in 1992. Frank Warren's sister Pat later asked her friends that any gifts intended for her forthcoming birthday should be given as financial donations to the Construction Safety Campaign to progress the work of the campaign.

Southwark DLO support for the Construction Safety Campaign

Our aim was to get unlawful killing verdicts and have cases reviewed by the Crown Prosecution Services (CPS). We went on to meet at these inquests many of the families of those killed.

UCATT Leadership attempts to discredit the Construction Safety Campaign

When UCATT's leadership found that support for the CSC was growing, UCATT leaders decided they would try to deter any further backing for the campaign.

The union's then general secretary, Albert Williams, wrote to all union branches on 4th May 1989 asking them to oppose any support for the campaign. Despite this many of its own branches and regional councils were beginning to give active support to the CSC. If anything, this letter enabled the CSC to get more support from UCATT branches and some UCATT regional councils. We held our first lobby of the Houses of Parliament on 9th October 1989.

Shown in the photo are some of the large numbers of Southwark building DLO workers on the CSC lobby of Parliament.

Southwark DLO support for the Construction Safety Campaign

These are, from left: George Amery, Dave Lindsell, Steve Matthews, Ade Onanigi. On the right-hand side at the back are two Southwark painter apprentices. Hundreds of workers attended.

London steel erectors shop stewards voted to call cabin meetings of their members to get them to take strike action on the day in support of the lobby, as did other construction trades workers on Canary Wharf, Broadgate and the Minster Court site.

Building Direct Labour workers were also represented with coach loads coming from Southwark and Hackney Building DLOs. Many others travelled from different parts of the UK. At the same time, the then UCATT leadership boycotted the lobby. Shortly after this lobby an early day motion was moved by Michael Meacher MP in support of the demands of the CSC which was supported by over 250 MPs.

International Workers' Memorial Day

The CSC on 28 April 1991 held the first major event in the UK for Workers Memorial Day. Ever since many others have been held each year.

This commemoration was first held 5 years earlier in Canada in 1986 when the Canadian Labour Congress designated 28 of April as a day of mourning for people killed or injured at work. United States trades unionists adopted this day in commemoration of workers who were killed in a construction accident in Connecticut in 1987.

Since then many others have adopted the Workers' Memorial Day. Finally, the TUC in Britain agreed to recognise the commemoration at its Congress held in 1999. Now many other trade unions in Europe recognise Workers' Memorial Day.

As the campaign began to grow from strength to strength in 1989 many UCATT regional councils were in open defiance of the leadership of the Union. One of the people who gave us a lot of support was that of the late Lol Irwin, Midlands regional secretary of UCATT. Lol gave us the use of the Midlands Regional Office to hold two public meetings.

CSC supporters attend the Durham Miners' Gala each year to link up with many others in this celebration of working-class solidarity.

The Durham Miners' Gala is the largest working-class event held in Europe and was reported in the press as having over 200,000 in attendance in 2017.

Southwark DLO support for the Construction Safety Campaign

The late Lol Irwin can be seen holding a banner at the Durham Miners' Gala

UCATT National Conference in May 1990 Reverses Opposition to CSC

In 1990, UCATT reversed its opposition to the CSC when four resolutions were put to the conference These were from Uxbridge UG226 Branch, Dalkeith UA068 Branch, Livingston UA365 Branch, and Liverpool UD386 Branch. After the 1990 UCATT National Conference, the leadership of the Union were keen to show their support for the campaign.

Relatives support group set up

In January 1992, a group of those who had lost relatives in the building industry and other workplaces formed the "Construction Deaths Relatives Support Group". Angela Riley, sister of a construction worker killed at Canary Wharf in East London became the secretary and Ann Elvin, mother of Paul Elvin who was killed at Euston railway station, was the group coordinator.

Southwark DLO support for the Construction Safety Campaign

Above can be seen the families of killed construction workers preparing to march from Euston Station to the House of Commons.

Fight to ban asbestos imports 1995 – 2000

Above is a picture of construction workers in 1976 on strike against the use of asbestos on the John Laing Barbican Arts Centre site in the City of London. First on the left is the late Jim Franklin, the union convenor; in 1988 he became the founding chairman of the Construction Safety Campaign. (44)

Southwark DLO support for the Construction Safety Campaign

In the year 2000, we produced a booklet entitled: "The FIGHT TO BAN ASBESTOS 1995 – 2000." Please read it for a much more detailed account of the events. (please see the last page of this book to order). One of the biggest achievements of the CSC was in 1996 when we successfully led the way in starting a national campaign to have asbestos imports banned from the UK. That did not mean that getting asbestos imports banned had ended the struggles over asbestos, as the fight to get asbestos already installed in properties removed continues today.

Workers' Memorial Day 2003. City of London protest

Our demonstration that year was led by a horse-drawn hearse, filled with hard hats, each one representing construction workers killed in this part of London. Our lead banner read "Murder Mile, because of the huge numbers of construction workers who had been killed within this one square mile of the City of London. This is largest financial area in Europe that was making enormous profits in offices built by these killed workers.

The person in the picture above holding the front banner is Ian Watt, at the time the asbestos removal worker shop steward in Southwark DLO. The names of those killed are shown on this banner.

156

Southwark DLO support for the Construction Safety Campaign

Above can be seen the construction workers who stopped work to march towards the Wembley National Football Stadium building site.

In 2004, hundreds of workers stopped work on the Wembley National Football Stadium site on "Workers' Memorial Day". They marched to remember Patrick O'Sullivan who was killed there in January 2004. They walked off the Wembley site down Olympic way to be joined by contingents of workers from all over London and as far afield as the Midlands. This was a tremendous historic event which showed the support of construction workers and the demands of the campaign. It was planned and organized by the CSC.

Increasing collapse of cranes

In September 2006, a Falcon crane on a Barrett's Building site in Battersea South West London collapsed killing Jonathan Cloke the crane driver and a member of the public, Michael Alexa. With the help of the CSC and the Battersea & Wandsworth Trades Council, the 'Battersea Crane Disaster Action Group' was set up; it held numerous protests, lobbies of Wandsworth Council and its MPs as well as lobbies of Parliament. It was also successful in getting the support of the then Labour Government to have an Act carried through Parliament for the registration of cranes. This was junked when the Tory Government was returned to power.

Southwark DLO support for the Construction Safety Campaign

It took ten years for the case over the deaths that resulted from this crane collapse to be heard at court. What a disgrace!

What Has the CSC Achieved?

The CSC's campaign activities have contributed to some very important developments:

1. Fewer construction workers are now killed than before the campaign started. 2018/2019 saw 30 deaths. In 1988 at the start of our campaign there were 157 deaths. (128)

2. We achieved a UK ban on the import and use of asbestos in 1999.

3. New laws for the safe management of asbestos in workplaces.

4. Far greater awareness of asbestos hazards.

5. Many employers have received substantial prison sentences over construction workers' deaths. Prior to the campaign, no employers had been jailed.

6. Fines by courts are much higher, in particular because of the use of Corporate Manslaughters laws, but these are still far too low.

7. Ill health and poor safety conditions are now more understood.

8. Workers Memorial Day, 28 April, established as a major event by the CSC in the UK in 1991 is now recognised as a major labour movement event.

9. In 1990s CSC actions helped to defeat the then Tory government's attempts to scrap the Health and Safety at Work Act.

10. The CSC was the first organisation that ensured the involvement of relatives of killed construction workers.

Southwark DLO support for the Construction Safety Campaign

The ongoing attacks made on Health and Safety since the book on the CSC was written in 2010

DOORSTEPPING: Tony O'Brien confronts Employment Minister Chris Grayling

Picture: Andrew Wiard

Angry protest follows ceremonies

by Paddy McGuffin
Home Affairs Reporter

MORE than one hundred events took place around Britain yesterday to commemorate Worker's Memorial Day.

In London construction and transport workers at an event in Tower Hill released black balloons to signify those who have died.

A roll call of those construction workers killed in the last year was also read out and a minute's silence held.

Later in the day furious union members protested out-

side the offices of the Department of Work and Pensions over the cuts to the HSE and public sector, which they argue will inevitably lead to more deaths.

Union reps confronted Employment Minister Chris Grayling, the architect of the HSE cuts that will lead to 11,000 fewer workplace inspections each year.

Speaking at the Tower Hill event Construction Safety Campaign national secretary Tony O'Brien, who took part in the DWP protest, said: "Why are they (the coalition government)

set on this path? They are not mad they are criminal. They know the consequences, they just don't care."

Commemorations were also held throughout England, Scotland and Wales including events in Bristol,

Coventry, Wolverhampton, Sheffield, Bradford, Manchester, Liverpool, Sunderland and Durham.

A number of events were also arranged in Edinburgh, Glasgow and Cardiff.

paddym@peoples-press.com

YEOVIL & DISTRICT
TRADES UNION COUNCIL
May Day 2011 celebration —
fight the cuts!
Friday April 29

TONIGHT

2011, Workers' Memorial Day saw Chris Grayling the then Tory Government Minister responsible for Health and Safety being confronted by me in a demonstration outside the offices of the Department of Work and Pensions.

In 2012, there was a huge 35% cut to the Health and Safety Executive budget. A Professor Lofstedt had shortly before recommended de-regulation of safety law involving changes to section 47 of the Health & Safety at Work Act.

Southwark DLO support for the Construction Safety Campaign

The changes reduced the civil liability of employers for breaches of Health and Safety regulations. Previously an injured employee could claim against the employer even if the employer (supposedly) had not done anything wrong.

The new legislation removed this "strict liability" and in future claims must be pursued under the common law of negligence. In other words, the claimant must prove that:

- the employer failed to provide a safe place and system of work.
- it was reasonably foreseeable that injury would result from this breach and that such an injury occurred.

These changes were for accidents occurring on or after 1st October 2013.

The other main changes recommended by Professor Lofstedt were:

- Exemption of so-called "low-risk" self-employed workers from the protection of health and safety laws, unless allowed for by a prescribed list.
- To continue to review all Approved Codes of Practice.
- Changes to the Construction (Design and Management) Regulations 2007.
- Make greater use of "so far as is reasonably practicable" criteria in safety.
- Removal of the Construction (Head Protection) Regulations 1989.
- Removal of the requirement for cranes to be registered.

In 2011, the Tory-led coalition government tried to denigrate health and safety with David Cameron's infamous reference to health and safety as a "monster". He also talked about "waging war against health and safety culture".

This shows how the health and safety of construction workers were denigrated and ignored. This vile propaganda from the Tories had a consequence for many others as it acted as a cover for the wholesale deregulation of house building that has affected social housing tenants. The consequence is the horror that took place in the Grenfell Tower in Kensington and Chelsea that claimed the lives of 71 people and seriously injured many others.

In 2014, the CSC together with UCATT and UNITE handed a letter of protest to the Qatar Embassy, demanding an end to the slaughter taking place on its sites. It was estimated 4,000 workers could die before the World Cup kicks off. A virtual slave labour system exists with migrant workers denied basic rights. We demanded this event should not take place unless the slaughter was stopped.

Southwark DLO support for the Construction Safety Campaign

Above: our protest at the Qatar Embassy

Above: our protest in 2014, over the death of Kevin Campbell, killed while working on a construction rail project next to the London Olympic Park.

Kevin's death came in the same month as a worker who was killed on the £15bn Crossrail project. A worker on Balfour Beatty's Providence tower site in London's docklands was also seriously injured after a crane collapse.

Pictured above is the protest and silent vigil held by the Construction Safety Campaign and others outside the court case into Rene Tkacik death.

On 12 April 2017, three construction firms appeared in court over the death of a worker and the injury to two others on London's Crossrail project.

Rene Tkacik died on 7 March 2014, after being crushed by falling concrete while working on the rail project's Fisher Street tunnel. BAM Nuttall, Ferrovial Agroman (UK), and Keir Infrastructure and Overseas each faced four charges of breaches of health and safety regulations. The case was referred to the higher-level Crown Court for a further hearing. At the Crown Court hearing on 28 July 2017 the contractors were fined a mere £300,000 for Tkakic's death but fined a total of £1million over many other unsafe incidents that had occurred at Crossrail. Campaigners expressed disappointment at the fine saying this will cost the three multinationals £100,000 each, which is probably less than the bonuses their senior managers will get on the project. (45)

On 21 April 2017. Contractor CMF was fined when 31-year-old Richard Laco died after being crushed by a large construction object at the Francis Crick Institute in London on 6 November 2013. CMF Ltd pleaded guilty, they were fined £185,000 and ordered to pay costs of £20,606.14. (51)

Southwark DLO support for the Construction Safety Campaign

Above is a picture of the protest held in November 2013 at the construction site where Richard Laco died.

Above is Southwark DLOs delegation at the 2016 Workers Memorial Day event held at Tower Hill

Southwark DLO support for the Construction Safety Campaign

Safety fines double

It was reported In May 2017, that in 2016 construction health and safety offences fines had reached £14m with four construction companies being charged over £1 million. Balfour Beatty Utility Solutions suffered the largest at £2.6 million last May after a trench collapse killed a worker. The increase in fines comes after sentencing guidelines were ratcheted up in February 2016. This demonstrates the importance of the Construction Safety Campaign which over the last 31 years has led the way in demanding a massive increase in what were in the past incredibly low fine levels. (52)

The above shows a £6,000 donation being presented at the CSC's AGM on 30th April 2017. Solicitor Helen Clifford presented this award from the family of Rene Tkacik, who was killed on the London Crossrail project. This award was made towards the work of the CSC in supporting families of loved ones who have been killed on construction sites

The UN-backed Rotterdam Convention of Nations held in May 2017 failed to agree a curb on the asbestos trade. This was after some countries had backed calls for chrysotile to be added to a list of dangerous substances.

Southwark DLO support for the Construction Safety Campaign

Asbestos remains a widely used building product particularly in the developing world. Russia, a leading asbestos producer, has blocked previous attempts to list the product, as has India. This is even though more than 50 nations, including all members of the EU, have banned all forms of asbestos. (53)

Successful court case exposes extent of Corporate Spying against Anti Asbestos Campaigners

A multinational covert operation mounted by asbestos industry to infiltrate and spy on the campaigning group the "Ban Asbestos Network" was settled in the courts in 2018.

The court case revealed how a public-school educated spy from Hertfordshire was tasked by a Mayfair-based intelligence agency to target Ban Asbestos activists. This resulted in legal action for breach of confidence, misuse of private information and breach of the Data Protection Act being launched in the London High Court against defendant Robert Moore, K2 Intelligence Ltd and K2's Executive Managing Director Matteo Bigazzi.

The court heard how elaborate details of how the claimants had been falsely befriended and spied upon.

Robert Moore spied on Kazan-Allen and her fellow Ban Asbestos colleagues in Britain and abroad and pocketed £336,000 in fees and £130,400 in expenses for his efforts. He obtained "highly confidential information" that was documented in thousands of files, 10 reports, photographs and recordings of private conversations and presentations which he had collected. Compensation was awarded in favour of five claimants.

Courts fail to act over blacklisting

May 2017: Dave Smith failed to win the blacklisting case he brought to the European Court of Human Rights (ECHR). It took eight years to bring the case through seven different courts to be ruled upon by the ECHR. From the start, Carillion admitted it used information on his blacklist file against him because he was a trade union member who had complained about safety on its building sites. Every judgement in the courts concluded he had "suffered a grave injustice" because of blacklisting.

You would have thought legal victory was assured. But in fact, he lost.

The reason? Because he was an agency worker, and thus not protected by UK law. (54)

Southwark DLO support for the Construction Safety Campaign

On 4 May 2017, Barroerock Construction Limited was fined £750,000 after failing to protect workers from asbestos contamination in Ashford, Kent. The first investigation resulted in up to 40 workers being exposed to asbestos. At the second investigation in June 2014 the company was unable to provide documentation to show that asbestos materials identified had been safely removed.

The company went into liquidation in February, despite its annual turnover of £10 million. This meant the £750,000 fine imposed will shamefully will only be added to the creditors. (55)

In May 2017, Bill Lawrence, secretary of the "Construction Safety Campaign" gave a report on his studies into the sinister practice of companies who spread asbestos throughout the world. His report shows that millions of tonnes a year are still mined and traded worldwide. The major producers are Russia, Kazakhstan, Brazil and China, all of whom ship the deadly dust to south-east Asia, and central and southern America. Bill revealed how millions of tonnes of asbestos production and export of asbestos is causing untold deaths worldwide while making vast profits, often through money laundering operations by offshore companies, Research showed half of the world's asbestos exports are traded by companies registered in the UK. (56)

On 30 June 2017, a construction manager, Andrew Winterton, was jailed for four years for manslaughter after the site death of Shane Wilkinson, 33, who was crushed to death when the wall of a trench collapsed while he was working on a building site in September 2014. Conquest Homes was sentenced to a fine of £55,000 plus £30,000 costs. (62)

Blacklist Support Group

The single most important achievement in recent years has been the success of the Blacklist Support Group – the campaign aimed at exposing and getting justice for construction workers who were denied work as a result of their trade union activities.

The group has campaigned tirelessly and finally must be written into history as the main force behind the trade unions and their own solicitors in winning over £75 million compensation for 771 out of the 3,200 blacklisted workers who came forward to be part of the High Court case in June 2016. These included prosecution of well-known construction companies such as McAlpine, Carillion, Laing O'Rourke, Skanska and Balfour Beatty.

Southwark DLO support for the Construction Safety Campaign

The companies' lawyer read out to a crowded courtroom what was described as an "unreserved and sincere" apology for the "distress and anxiety" caused to the workers and their families. The statement was interrupted by Dave Smith of the Blacklist Support Group and co-author of the book "Blacklisted", who shouted:

"Under no circumstances do we consider this to be a sincere apology". He was backed by 40 other blacklisted workers who chanted 'No justice, No peace.'

The Blacklist Support Group is still campaigning for a public inquiry to expose the full scale of the blacklisting scandal. (54)

See above one of the many protests held by the Blacklist Support Group outside the High Court in London

The Creedon Report

In March 2019 the Police admitted to the Blacklist Support Group that they had passed information about trade unionists to employers which had resulted in the blacklisting of workers. The previously secret 69-page report was compiled by senior police officer Mick Creedon in 2016; it followed allegations that for years the police Special Branch had monitored political activists and shared personal funded and organised by major construction companies.

According to the report the police have had specific units to monitor trade unionists and liaised with blacklisting companies for decades.

Southwark DLO support for the Construction Safety Campaign

What a disgraces after fighting to get asbestos banned in the UK in the years 1995-1999 - 20 years later we still suffer the same 50,000 deaths each year

2019 marks 20 years since we got asbestos banned in Britain. Yet, asbestos remains the largest killer from occupation disease in our country, killing thousands every year.

We achieved a ban on the use of asbestos as well as far greater workplace asbestos protection laws after the CSC and many others waged a sustained campaign in March 1995 when it was announced there had been a dramatic increase in asbestos related fatalities. This came after many years in which 100,000s of UK workers have been killed, this happened despite the warnings of a British Factory inspector over 100 years ago of "the evil effects of it" and what was a last ditch stand counter lobby against it being banned by big business interests in 1999.

Yet today, huge numbers are still dying from asbestos. We now must demand that money is made available so that a national wide UK asbestos survey is carried out and for this to be followed up by a full programme for its safe removal in all dwellings.

Without workers' rights there will be no sustained, long-term improvements to health and safety at work

1. We must be able to take direct action against unsafe employers as this is far better than waiting around for courts to make decisions. Laws will always predominantly favour employers.

2. Health and Safety standards laid down by law are only minimum standards. Workers must aim to achieve agreements which are far better than these minimum standards.

3. Safety at work is all about maximising workers' ability to control the workplace to prevent and minimise the abusive and exploitative power of the employers.

4. We must have the right to refuse dangerous work without being victimised.

5. We must have rights to take any form of industrial action including strike action without anti-trade union laws being used to take court action against us.

Southwark DLO support for the Construction Safety Campaign

6. We must have the right to be directly employed instead of being treated as having little or no rights by being falsely deemed self-employed.

7. We must have the right not to be blacklisted for any reason whatsoever.

8. The right of full-time employment must be fully achieved by having existing council run DLOs expanded with new ones set up together with the founding of a publicly controlled national construction company.

9. Tiredness kills, so we must reduce working hours without any loss of pay.

10. We must have decent rates of pay, pensions and fully paid holidays (not rolled up holiday pay) sick and industrial injury pay.

Our Fight for Direct Labour Employment

The Case for Council Building Direct Labour Organisation

Over many years Southwark building DLO stewards put our case to Southwark council that we should not just maintain our work, but it should be expanded. Similar arguments, where they apply, could be used for the expansion of many other DLOs – some of these arguments are shown below.

Southwark Building Services

Southwark building services provides a complete reactive and planned building maintenance service. We have operated over many years operating a 365-day service, carrying out work in 1980 to over 60,000 council properties and in 2019 to over 30,000 of Southwark's properties. While our main contract is with Southwark Housing, we also worked with tenant management organisations, joint management boards, and public and education departments within Southwark.

- We now carry out all of Southwark's repairs and maintenance work.
- We have worked closely with the Council to deliver its improvements.

Benefits from having Council directly employed workers

The council's direct labour workforce provides accountability and skills not matched by contractors. This is in complete contrast to contractors who subcontract large amounts of their work. The council's own workers are directly employed, being fully legally qualified for electrical, gas, asbestos removal, roofing, metal fitting, plumbing, bricklaying, plastering, carpentry joinery, painting and decorating work.

Apprentice training to Southwark tenants and residence

The council's Direct Building Services can be proud of the fact that it has trained hundreds of local young people to become skilled tradespersons.

Profits made by contractors

Money made by handing work to contractors goes directly to directors' and shareholders' pockets whereas by retaining the council's own Direct Labour Organisation means the council and its tenants will continue to benefit from the tens of millions of pounds in surpluses that had already gone back to the council to provide for more services over the many years since the DLO has existed..

The Case for Council Building Direct Labour Organisation

Unsafe contractors

Contractors who had worked for Southwark had an appalling safety record. In July 2017, Kier, contractors to the Crossrail project being built in central London, were fined over £1m over the death of a worker and two other unsafe incidents; its parent company already had 12 Prohibition and Improvement Notices imposed by the Health and Safety Executive (HSE). In December 2017 Kier was also fined £1.8 M over the death of a worker from its construction site at Lidgate, Newmarket in 2014.

Morrison had five Prohibition and Improvement Notices laid against them by the HSE and on two separate occasions they were found guilty of failing to comply with Health and Safety Law which then led to the deaths of two workers.

Instability and uncertainties of Contractors

The use of contractors brings instability in the provision of continuous services. Botes Ltd who in 1996 had worked for Southwark and had carried out 45% of the council's repairs and maintenance work. This company went into liquidation leaving council tenants, its creditors and workers to suffer the consequences.

Dangers of price fixing and no control

The council's Building Direct Labour Organisations has been successfully used to prevent private sector contractors gaining a monopoly of the council's work and all that goes with it, such as collusion between contractor's contract-rigging, and inflated prices. If the DLO is lost it is Southwark tenants that will suffer by having to pay the increased costs.

Lack of safety and quality work standards

In contrast to the council's Building DLO, contractors did not have fully equipped building repairs and maintenance depots. There needs to be pre-contract scrutiny on all contractors before they are taken on to carry out what can potentially be very dangerous work, e.g. activities such as stores supply and working areas, asbestos containment and handling of other dangerous wastes, from carpenter/joinery, machinery workshop and glass- cutting workshop operations.

There was no let-up in a long history of contractors ripping-off Southwark Council as well as other Local Authorities

We said on many occasions that there are contractors who collude with other contractors when they put in tenders to carry out Southwark's work.

The Case for Council Building Direct Labour Organisation

They collaborate in price-fixing, and after being awarded work they are masters at bumping-up prices. They will do this at the expense of the council ratepayer and the conditions of the workers they engage to carry out their work.

17 January 2008

The National Audit Office revealed that millions of pounds of taxpayers' money is being wasted by officials who overpay private firms to do the simplest tasks, such as installing a new electric socket or replacing a lock. An investigation into £180 million of public money revealed a 10-fold difference in payments for similar tasks.

17 April 2008

The Office of Fair Trading' named 112 construction companies which it says colluded to inflate the cost of a wide range of contracts.

Some of the largest construction companies are on this list, including companies which carried out work for Southwark, and continue to do so today. These are: Beazer (now known as Kier), Connaught, and Apollo. In addition to these contractors there will be many more such companies which are included on Southwark's approved list for tendering. **In September 2009 Kier was found guilty by the Office of Fair Trading for price fixing and fined £17,894.438. At that time, this was the highest fine made against a major contractor.**

20 June 2008

The South London press reported:

Southwark suspends four employees while it carries out fraud investigations."
"Finance staff were alerted to suspicious financial transactions after the Housing Department was disbanded in 2006.

"It was feared that bogus companies have been set up and funds channelled to them for work to Southwark's housing stock that was never carried out."

Measures required for construction

No matter which political party is in national or local government, the inefficiency, corruption and exploitation of the workers in the private sector of the construction industry must be exposed and fought against. Alongside this, we must strive to get new DLOs created and get existing ones to expand.

However, we must recognise that change in the leadership of the Labour Party has opened the potential for major gains to be made for workers. We need to reverse what has been the exploitation of construction workers by the employers, as up to now the private contractors have mainly had their way.

Measures required for construction

Now, we have an entirely new situation. The Tory government is more vulnerable, having been humiliated at the last general election and having to rely on the Ulster Unionists to survive. How then have things changed? We cannot allow this opportunity to go unanswered, when we know that out of all the main political party leaderships Labour is more supportive towards our aims.

We also know that nothing comes without a fight against those within Labour that are still carrying out the Tory's policies, particularly over social housing within local authorities. These policies must now be reversed, but change doesn't happen on its own; it will have to be fought for.

We cannot just wait for a Labour Government to be elected, or a change in the attitude by many Labour councillors and MPs. We must demand they act now. We need decisions from Local Authorities to expand their Direct Labour Organisations where they currently exist and start the process of setting them up where they don't.

The need to persuade councils to support DLOs

We need to act to expose and prevent the truly unfair competition that takes place between private contractors and local authority DLOs under the government's biased regulations.

Councils lack contract compliance officers. This needs to change with far greater use being made of spot-checks by unannounced visits by officers to ensure that work is being done in accordance with the contract because:

1. Contractors are good at submitting false bids for local authority work. They do this in many ways. One way is by robbing building workers of proper pay and working conditions.

    Councils have a responsibility to prevent this. They can also prevent the tax evasion that contractors get away with by their use of umbrella companies and other-cheating methods. This robs councils of the funds they need to carry out their vital services.

2. Contractors put in tenders for work based on lost leaders (lost leaders are low prices put in by contractor to win work. They then will go on to make exaggerated claims that enable prices for work to be inflated that enables them to secure far greater amounts of money over the long term period within contracts) They also do this so as to offset overheads when they have lower periods of work. Councils must stop this practice by designing contracts to prevent these loss-leader bids.

Measures required for construction

3. DLOs need to be allowed to tender for new building work outside their own authority. Being unable to compete in many areas that are open to private contractors is an unfair restraint.

4. On many types of jobs DLOs should be awarded work without having to go through a tendering process. This could be done when it is deemed the DLO is evaluated as "best value".

5. Local authorities should extend the existing work of DLOs based on previous satisfactory performance of their contracts.

6. Trades unions and tenants' bodies should be represented right from the very start when setting up contracts. This should include them being on their council's contracts evaluation teams, being able to make verbal and written observations and have these considered at all stages of the process, including: the setting up of the contracts, invitation to tender, short listing, tender evaluations and recommendation of officers to council for the award of contracts.

7. Repair and maintenance contracts should be fully integrated with other council services and deliver a quality product. Councils need to recognise that this type of set-up can only be fully achieved by using a DLO rather than contractors.

8. Vigorous pre-tender examination of contract bidders must take place, with contractors only being allowed on the approved list of contractors after they have been subject to a vigorous test to reveal their record; i.e. whether they have abused laws on the protection of workers' rights and the environment.

9. The wording within contracts must be explicit, no doubt should be left as to what they mean.

10. Letters must be sent out to all contractors who have submitted tenders to oblige them to guarantee they will meet all the costs associated with Direct Labour's pay and terms and conditions. These conditions must be guaranteed prior to any transfer of DLO workers should such contractors win a contract. Evaluation of their estimates must be closely scrutinised so that bogus non-TUPE tenders are eliminated.

11. vigorous on-site safety inspections must take place to eliminate the use of unsafe contractors.

Measures required for construction

12. Suspect performance targets by existing contractors must not be allowed to count for reference of competence.

13. thorough pre-contract award external checks must be carried out on contractors.

14. cost must not be the primary factor when deciding on a contract award.

15. the use by councils of consultants must cease.

16. the practice of using contractor management teams to manage DLOs must end.

17. contractors must not be allowed to subcontract their work.

18. those tendering for work must be able to demonstrate their history of:

    a. viability.

    b. of interests.

    c. track record and tribunal findings.

    d. records, including any warnings or prosecutions by the HSE.

    e. employing workers directly and that they will continue doing so.

    f. a proven history of apprentice and adult training schemes.

    g. having all the required depot facilities, parking and workshops.

19. The contractor must be able to show as a minimum that they have the same safety provisions as the council. They must be able to demonstrate their Health and Safety viabilities. The following are not exclusive examples:

    a. Health and Safety Management system.

    b. risk assessments in place and control of risk assessments.

    c. training and qualification records: Asbestos, Manual Handling, COSHH, Gas, Roofing, Scaffolding, Safety certification, CSCS card. Electrical qualifications and all other trades training and qualifications.

    d. asbestos database and management of asbestos safety systems.

    e. monitoring requirements for all work.

20. DLOs must be able to demonstrate to councils the advantages to keeping work in-house, for example:

    a. workers who are directly employed have long-service reliability and are well tested for security purposes.

Measures required for construction

b. DLO workers have lots of experience with council properties and customer care while those employed by contractors are mostly not directly employed.

c. DLOs acts against contractor collusion and anti-competition ringing practices to inflate contract prices.

d. DLOs acts against profit motive driven contractors and any surpluses made by DLOs go back to councils who can use it to provide for more work to be carried out.

e. Safety records of DLOs are far superior to that of contractors with a healthy input by well qualified safety trade union representatives with safety committee structures playing a major role in preventing accidents at work.

f. Ongoing customer care, including various safety training: CSCS Card, Gas, Electrical, Asbestos as well as having a high level of the DLO workforce as apprentice trainees.

g. DLOs workers are in the main employed on very similar or the same terms and conditions as opposed to contractors' workers who will be subject to various forms of employment abuse including different types of contracts of employment, being claimed as self-employed or agency workers. The current main abuse is being part of the umbrella company scam which subjects' workers to all sorts of cuts to their pay. All this acts to deny workers their employment rights.

h. Can provide long-lasting, sustainable, quality and environmentally friendly construction products with its own workshops. Having these produced with the use of high standards of health and safety.

i. DLOs have a public duty to promote equality and have policies which act against all forms of discrimination.

Solutions needed from the Government for the Construction Industry

Councils must be allowed to put to work the hundreds of thousands of unemployed construction workers and have large-scale quality apprentice training programmes. This can be done by establishing major house building, renovation and maintenance programmes.

A future Labour Government must set up a publicly owned and controlled National Building Direct Labour Organisation to spearhead its plans for a large-scale house building programme.

Measures required for construction

This publicly owned National Housing Building Organisation will in addition to carrying out public sector work, be allowed to tender for all private sector new build and housing repair and maintenance work.

A new Labour Government must also immediately bring in the following new robust legislation that will:

The purpose of producing the above list is to highlight the need for changes desperately needed for both workers in building DLOs and for those who work in the private sector of the construction industry.

I don't claim that this is an exclusive list as there will be many supporters of these changes who I would welcome to make additional proposals.

The main thing is that we need to raise the arguments to a much higher level. We need to pass resolutions at union branches, Labour Party meetings and most importantly for them to be put into practise.

- Remove all anti-DLO competitive tendering legislation.

- End the practice of price-fixing and contract-rigging. This would enable DLOs to tender for its work on an equal playing field, thereby creating far better cost and quality UK housing. Companies found guilty of price-fixing would need to be prosecuted and barred from public sector contracts.

- Bar companies found guilty of blacklisting from future public-sector contracts. Directors of companies found guilty of blacklisting should face jail, be fined and barred from holding any future directorships of companies.

- Rescind the right of companies to refuse employment at industrial tribunals of workers who had been sacked because of their membership of trades unions or campaigning activities for workers' rights and allow these workers the option of reinstatement or enhanced compensation.

- End the use of umbrella companies.

- Define what is genuine direct employment and genuine self-employment.

- Guarantee the employment protection rights of all workers with no exclusions allowed whatsoever by companies or employment agencies.

- Set up talks with the trades unions for reaching agreement on how laws concerning workers' employment rights, health and safety, and industrial actions can be greatly strengthened.

Council Housing

My relationship as a tenant with Council Housing

My father Michael O' Brien came over from Ireland with his brother James during the second world war. He was part of a workforce of those from Ireland who responded to calls for assistance to carry out the repairs of boats for the Dunkirk evacuation of France in 1940. He went on to carry out work on motorway bridges, council housing and prefabricated properties. Like many in those years who came over from Ireland, despite the huge contribution that Irish building workers were making towards the reconstruction of Britain, being Irish, meant you were not that welcome. After living out of site caravans on motorways Dad and Uncle James had many housing refusals and were desperate so were forced to stay for several weeks in what was a homeless person's complex (The Spike) in Bournemouth Road, Peckham.

My Mom first met Dad at a St Patricks day celebration at the Swan Pub in Stockwell Brixton and shortly after they were married. They were desperate to have their own housing after being forced to live in an overcrowded house with her Mom and Dad in Brixton.

Many homes were left empty after the second world war. This was largely due to those being killed and injured and some who had resettled in areas where they were evacuated. This enabled my Dad to find a vacant house in Blake's Road, Peckham. I was born in St Giles Hospital in Southwark in 1948 and for 11 years grew up in the Blake's Road house. It was one of several thousand in Southwark that would now be regarded as slum terrace housing: no electricity, only gas lighting, coal fires for heating, no bathroom, and only an outside toilet. Within a short time, our home, alongside many others in our area, was taken over by Southwark Council. Apart from a brief period in Ireland after our grandfather died, I lived in this house until I was 12 years old.

My relationship as a tenant with Council Housing

Above is a picture outside our house in Ballybunion County Kerry Ireland. From left to right are: Me, my Dad, Brothers Denis and Michael.

Housing conditions in many parts of rural Ireland then in the early 1950s were very primitive. This house had had no electricity or gas and very little water sanitation.

During our time in Southwark, our house (and others lived in by several other family members from Ireland) was used to house the extended family, the three bedrooms were often shared by six to ten family members. This overcrowding was typical for many working-class families after the second world war.

In the 1960s, the council was undertaking a huge demolition programme to make way for several large council estates in Southwark's North Peckham and Walworth area. This enabled us to get a transfer to a three-bedroom house in Lyndhurst grove. An old terrace property with a back yard facing a railway track, but at least it had electricity, a small bathroom and an inside toilet. Amazingly, at that time, every three years you also got the inside and outside of your property redecorated by the council. But we still suffered from a lack of space and I still had to share a bedroom with one of my brothers.

My relationship as a tenant with Council Housing

Dad made many complaints to the council about this lack of space and later was told we could choose a move to one of three council houses on offer. What a comparison from what happens today when you would be very lucky to get any housing offers.

We chose to move to the huge North Peckham estate in 1970. At last, after living in a Southwark Council property for over 22 years, I didn't have to share a bedroom with my brothers. Our new home was the first one to be fully equipped with all the modern facilities, it was energy efficient, having central heating, double glazing, a new bathroom and kitchen. A year later I moved out of my council home after meeting my then partner Kathy. Kathy and I were unable to obtain council housing as we were outside of the councils housing criteria, being young, single and living outside the home of Mom and Dad.

My housing fortunes had reversed as we ended up living in a damp infected house that was plagued by rats. Its windows were rotten, and its staircase was falling apart. We had to share the one bathroom and kitchen with two other couples. We made a complaint to the council's environmental health department who paid us a visit and ordered the landlords to make major improvements to the property. This luckily enabled us in 1974 to become a priority applicant on Lewisham councils housing waiting list and we were then able to obtain a one-bedroom council flat at Milford Towers in Catford.

Shortly after my dad died in 1975, we got married and needed larger accommodation to start a family. This proved difficult to achieve from the council, so we ended up having to get a mortgage from the then GLC that enabled us to get a run-down house in the street next to Mom in Nunhead, Southwark.

My own personnel experience with council housing between 1948-1975 showed that for a large part of my life while it was never easy, at least you had some hope of having council housing. Compare that today with greatly reduced housing being built in both the public and private sector, with so many council housing tenants being driven out of properties because of demolition and privatisation and not being able to afford accommodation elsewhere. This shows how things have massively worsened.

Aspects of Council Housing History

Council Housing History

There has been a major change over the last 40 years when home ownership of housing has become the main tenure, as it now represents over 60% of England's grossly inflated bubble of net worth. Yet this change has done so much to damage our quality of life. A huge amount of our income is now being spent for us to be housed compared with 40 years ago. We are denied our freedoms and our safety when so many people cannot afford housing, when this insecurity leads to a huge increase in poverty and to our physical and mental health. (79)

Council housing rents especially in the early years of council housing was not cheap and was mainly provided for better paid workers. At times governments have forced councils to put up rents. Yet, overall it has provided far lower rental and far better-quality homes than that provided by the private sector, but only because council tenants had been prepared to fight against their rents being increased. Today, the main mechanisms used to attack both private and public sector tenants' rents' have included cuts to: "Housing rent subsidies" (housing benefit), cuts to the more secure "Assured tenancies" and Protected tenancies. While at the same time they have increased the use of the less secure: "Assured shorthold tenancies", "Flexible fixed term tenancies" and "Starter tenancies". (76)

In 1960. UK home ownership was at 45% and council housing at 27%. Yet in 2017 home ownership had increased to 63% while council housing had dropped to 7%.

The result of this policy of running down council housing has seen a huge inflationary rise in the costs of private housing purchase, a major increase in the costs of private rental housing and the transfer of huge amounts of council homes to precarious Housing Associations. (107)

What is Council Housing

Council housing first came about due to a general acceptance that the private sector was unable to provide adequate housing for all and so state intervention was required so that good quality affordable housing could be provided. Council housing in this country has been largely determined by central government policies and legislation. Most politicians in the first three quarters of the twentieth century advocated a need to build more houses in the face of shortages in the post war periods, and the need to replace old designated slum areas of cities.

Council Housing History

While social housing is supplied from local authority council housing, it is also provided by not-for-profit Registered Social Landlords (RSLs) including Housing Associations. However, the definition of "social housing" is greatly undermined by the misleading term now widely used of "affordable housing" (in effect unaffordable housing provided at up to 80% of the housing market cost).

The role of Housing Associations has completely changed from once being the first providers of social housing, to over the last 40 years being used by Governments to transfer council homes to them and being the supplier of new housing based on affordable (that is unaffordable) rental housing and privately-owned homes. Consequently, Housing Associations are now defined by the Government as: **"Private Registered Providers (PRPs)"**

Some important events in fighting for council housing

The impetus for changes to take place to housing begun when Britain's cities began to expand during the nineteenth century growth of industrialisation. The inadequate housing built at this time was largely carried out by profit-seeking private builders at rents that workers could not afford. Then, most workers continued to live in slums or could end up in workhouses. While a small minority of the elderly population were able to obtain charitable Alms housing.

Our success – A History of fighting for council housing

1890. Housing of the Working Classes Act - allowed London's local councils to build houses as well as clearing away slums. This was the real start of councils providing people with houses for rent although very few were built before World War One. (31)

1900. Housing of the Working Classes Act extended the 1890 act to areas outside London. Councils could buy land outside their own district. Then workers were beginning to get themselves organised in trade unions (membership over two million) and were placing increasing demands for housing. Some of these main events were:

In 1891 A rent strike in London's East End helped win the Dockers Strike. (82) (84)

1912-1915. Tenants organised a wave of rent strikes across the country against high rents when the Labour Party led the protests in a campaign for public housing. (82)

Some important events in fighting for council housing

1914: In early January around 300 tenants living in the Burley area of Leeds went on rent strike against a 6 pence increase in rents imposed by the landlords. The strike lasted eight weeks. In the end, committee members had been evicted and blacklisted from renting any other home in the area. (86) Around 24,000 council homes had been built before 1914. (67)

1915. Great Glasgow rent strikes

Above can been seen Glasgow rent strike protesters.

In Glasgow During the Irish Land War of the 1880s and during the First World War landlords took advantage of the absence of the men who were at "the front" to raise the rents. The women left behind faced rent increase of up to 25% and would be forcibly evicted by bailiffs if they failed to pay. There was a popular backlash and 20,000 tenants went on rent strike. These strikes became an overwhelming success and spread to other cities throughout the UK and led to the government, on 27th November 1915 introducing legislation to restrict rents to the pre-war levels.

During the rent strike committees were formed. Cards were printed with the words 'RENT STRIKE. WE ARE NOT REMOVING.' and placed in the windows of houses where rent increases were demanded.

Some important events in fighting for council housing

Women would sit with a bell and keep close watch and whenever the Bailiff's officer appeared to evict a tenant; the bells were ringing to inform other women who came to where the alarm was being raised. They would hurl flour bombs and other missiles at the bailiff, forcing him to make a hasty retreat. It is said they even pulled down his trousers to humiliate him! (87)

18 tenants were prosecuted for non-payment. Thousands of women together with thousands of shipyard and engineering workers marched on the court. The Court felt alarmed at the sheer size of this peaceful demonstration. They 'phoned Lloyd George, at the time a minister in the wartime coalition government. He told them to release the tenants and promised he would act. Less than a month later Parliament passed the Rent Restriction Act, the first of its kind in Europe, setting rents for the duration of the war and six months to follow at pre-war levels. (88)

Clyde rent strikes resume

With the end of the war the government could not simply repeal the rent control measures brought about by the struggle on the Clyde. So, it recommended that graduated increases should be made. These were enacted and paid in most parts of the country, but they were opposed along the Clyde, and by December 1922, the Clyde tenants fought a prolonged and skilful legal battle in the courts, but the strike petered out through 1926. This prolonged rent strike was less dramatic than those of 1915, but, if nothing else, it seems that the tenants of Clydebank retained by their action several tens of thousands of pounds which they would otherwise have paid in increased rent. (83)

The Tudor Walter recommendations

The 1918 Tudor Walters Committee on the standards of post war local authority housing were revolutionary. The report recommended that working-class should have homes built with wider frontages and grouped around open spaces which would form recreation grounds, that they should have three bedrooms, a large living room, a scullery fitted with a bath and a separate WC.

With the country facing war things had changed dramatically as the ruling class was worried that here was a real fear of serious social unrest, even of the spread of the Russian Revolution led by the Bolsheviks. This fear gradually persuaded all political parties of the urgent need for housing social reforms. (85)

Some important events in fighting for council housing

Most pre-1919 corporation housing was built cheaply in high-density flats with small rooms and limited facilities including shared kitchen and toilets and no running hot water. Typical rents where high and did not provide housing for the very poor. It was not until the end of the First World War that many council housing was built. (83) (89)

The "Addison Act"

The 1919 Addison Act was a major step forward in housing provision. It made housing a national responsibility, and local authorities were given the task of developing new housing and rented accommodation.

Local authorities surveyed housing needs and carried out plans for provision of new council housing. **This was the beginning of council housing, as it was the state for the first-time taking responsibility for provision of working-class housing. Almost 4 million new houses were built between 1919 and 1939. 1,112 million were built by local authorities.** (83)

The type of conditions that led to the introduction of the 'Addison Act' saw 200 infants out of every 1000 die at birth or in their first year. (Today the figure is around 7 in every 1000). (84)

The Wheatley Act

1924. The Labour Party came to office for the first time and the Housing Act (Wheatley) was introduced. The act increased the subsidy to local authorities which were building houses. The high building standards embraced in 1919 were gradually reduced during the 1920s and 1930s, as cost considerations became paramount. A new three-bedroom house was often only 620 square feet compared to over 1000 square feet in 1919. The Wheatley Act remained in operation until 1933. In the ten years from 1924 to 1934, 493,000 'Wheatly' houses had been built by local authorities. 31% of the total housing built since 1919 was then council housing. (85)

1939. 1.1 million council homes were built in the inter-war years between 1918-1939 compared to fewer than 30,000 in the past two decades since 1995. (83)

1942. While the Beveridge Report was known for its recommendations which went on to establish the NHS, it also promised a huge post-war house building programme and rent controls in the private rental sector. (95)

1944 Housing Manual (Dudley Report) set new, higher specifications for housing. Cooking facilities had previously been in the living room and were moved into kitchens. Flats were to include sunny balconies where possible. (111)

Some important events in fighting for council housing

1945. The end of the 2nd world war saw the Labour Party introduce the largest programme of house building that had ever been carried out. In the decade after 1945, 1.5 million homes had been completed. Council renting had increased from 10% in 1938 to 26% in 1961. While In 1945. 26% of houses were owner-occupied, this had increased: 1950 29%, 1966 47%, 1970 49% 1983 63%. This sharply contrasted to the 10% of houses which were owner occupied in 1914. (80)

1946. Over 40,000 families occupied former army camps and empty homes from Yorkshire to the South Coast in a wave of squatting. Squatters' groups formed federations and called for more affordable housing. (82)

1948. Tenants Associations developed on the new council estates and new towns. National Association of Tenants & Residents formed (NATR) in 1948. (82)

1951. A Conservative government was elected when labour failed to meet its target of 240,000 homes a year. Lower standards were introduced, but the Tories continued the massive council house building programme of Labour. They promise 300,000 houses a year. They built 319,000 and by 1953 they exceeded this with a record 348,000. (83)

1953. We spent on average, 8.8% on housing expenditure in 1953 compared to 16.8% in 1983. In 2016 costs varied widely throughout the UK. but averaged 50% for housing. (85) While Londoners are now spending nearly two-thirds of their average income on rent as sky-high prices put even more homes out of reach. (122)

1956. Labour-controlled Woolwich Council built 4,473 council homes in 1956 almost 3,000 of them were built by its own DLO workforce. (67)

1957. Was a pivotal moment when between 1957 to 1964 the Conservatives abandon support for council housing and returned to their traditional support for private rents. They ended council subsidies, encouraged sales and ended many rent controls in the private rented sector – the effect was Rachmanism. Named after the landlord who raised rents and used thugs to carry out various criminal activities to intimidate and evict his tenants in the Notting hill area of north London. (31)

Some important events in fighting for council housing

A crowd defends Keniston House during the 1960 rent strike

The St Pancras rent rebellion battle

1959. While some Labour councils continued to build and resisted putting up their rents. In London in May 1959 the Tory party won control of St Pancras council and proceeded to put up the rents. Tenants decided to resist the increases under the slogan (which had been popular on the Clyde in 1915) "not a penny on the rents". Out of the 4,200 or so tenants affected 1,400 had not paid the increases. Eviction notices were issued against two tenants, one the secretary of the United Tenants-Association. Both men barricaded themselves and their families into their flats.

They were later ejected by bailiffs supported by large numbers of police, amid violent scuffles. This strike received sympathetic industrial action by council painters and Covent Garden porters. Staff at a nearby railway goods depot went on a 24-hour strike in support, a hundred men came from the Shell office building site on London's South Bank and led a march of between one and two thousand people to the Town Hall.

50 people were arrested, five of whom were later sent to prison. The council eventually succeeded in reaching agreement that accumulated arrears would be paid off by the defaulting tenants. (92)

Some important events in fighting for council housing

The Parker Morris report

1961. The Parker Morris Report introduced new standards, more space, better heating and improved kitchens. This led to more low-rise terraced housing, through rooms/open plan, three bedrooms and large windows; this style was much used in New Towns. (113)

1964. Harold Wilson narrowly won the election and rapid building of council housing was a major priority. It aimed to build 500,000 houses a year by 1970, but the economic crisis (?) and devaluation meant this figure was quietly dropped. (112)

1965. Summary evictions were abolished with the Rent Act of 1965 which gave security of tenure in unfurnished accommodation and introduced a scheme for assessment of fair rents. Between 1965 and 1969 1.8 million homes were built. 50% of them by local authorities. (103)

1966. Ken Loach's film "Cathy Come Home" caused outrage over appalling housing conditions that families faced in 1966. 'Cathy Come Home' did much to raise awareness of needs for decent homes for all the people. (104)

1967. 160,000 council homes were built, many being flats and tower blocks of poor design, but the new estates replaced appalling housing, and reduced private rented sector to around 10%. (82)

1968. Nationally there were 31% of council house tenants. The Conservative Greater London Council started a 70% three-year increase in council rents. 11,000 families went on rent strike. Labour councils introduced means testing. Tenants demanded better safety standards after the gas explosion at Ronan Point in Newham, London, killing four people. There were also rent strikes in Sheffield, Walsall and Liverpool. (82) (31)

1969. Labour returned on the promise of a rent freeze. The rent rebate system was modified but it fragmented and divided tenants as was predicted. (31)

1960s - 1970s. Was a time of Labour, Liberal and Trade Union patronage. The housing corruption scandals involving T Dan Smith a Labour leader in the North East of England, John Poulson a Liberal politician and Andrew Cunningham, a senior figure in the General and Municipal Workers' Union and the Labour Party. All of them went to prison for the large sums they made from their corrupt dealings with building contractors.

Some important events in fighting for council housing

Reginald Maudling who was then the Home Secretary and in charge of the police and a friend of Poulson's became chairman of one of his companies and was paid £5,000 per annum. In July 1972, the Police began an investigation for fraud. This precipitated the resignation of Reginald Maudling. This showed how privilege and elitism was rife and exposed the extent of what had been happening in the late 1960s and early 1970s (93)

1970. Ted Heath returns with a Tory government and a right-wing agenda which included forcing 'fair (private market) rents' on council tenants and means testing. (84)

1972. The Tory government brought in the '1972 Housing Finance Act' in addition to the right-to-buy, was the first major attempt by the Tories to hand over social housing to the private sector. The Act provoked a wave of protests. A rebellion by Labour councillors in Clay Cross was abandoned by Labour, despite many council areas giving support.

On 9th October 1972. 3,000 tenants in Kirkby went on a 14 month rent strike against the Housing Finances Act. The cause was a £1 increase in rent. (84)

1975. There were estimates of 10,000 to 50,000 organised squatters living in abandoned private and public housing. This led to Housing Co-operatives being formed. (82)

1976. Campaigns had forced Labour to pass the Race Relations Act in 1976, which brought in many tenants who had been excluded. (82)

1977. A Labour Government introduced the Housing (Homeless Persons) Act, which made it a duty of local authorities to provide accommodation for the registered homeless; this also includes the 1965 protections from evictions and unfair rent. At the same time Labour encouraged home ownership. (54%) (82)

1979. 42% of the British population were now living in local authority housing. This was just before Thatcher became prime minister on the 3rd May 1979. She then immediately begun to stop grants for council housing and puts limits on ability of councils to borrow. (102)

Governments acts against Council Housing

The Right to Buy

In 1980 the Thatcher Conservative Government brought in their version of the 'Right to Buy'. This was based on huge discounts and 100% mortgages. This became a major incentive towards persuading council tenants to buy their homes from their local authority. The origins of the idea of Right-to-Buy came from the Labour Party in the 1950s.

Governments acts against Council Housing

Right-to-Buy led to most better-quality council properties being purchased by the "sitting" tenants at a low price (this policy aimed at taking housing out of the public sector). At the same time spending restrictions were introduced that meant it was no longer possible to build new houses in large numbers. After fifty years of virtually uninterrupted growth, the numbers of council houses began to fall, and this has continued ever since.

1985. The 1985 Housing Act' introduced Large Scale Voluntary Transfer (LSVT). At first LSVT failed to take off and in fact under the Tories most of councils transferring to Housing Associations (RSL's) were in rural areas. (67)

1988. The 1988 Housing Act' introduced "Tenants Choice" which gave council tenants the right to transfer their homes to other social housing providers in practise this meant to Housing Associations. Housing Action Trusts (HAT) were brought into areas which the government identified needing improvement that resulted in the tenants being removed from council ownership. A House of Lords amendment forced a ballot on any transfer to a HAT. This allowed tenant campaigns to stop thousands of council houses from being transferred. (90)

1989. The 1989 Housing Finance Act 'ring-fenced' a Housing Revenue Account in Local Authorities. While at the same time they banned any Council Tax contributions towards housing and made sure very few profits on sales were used on housing, and milked rent income for Housing Benefit. This was exposed by tenants' 'Daylight Robbery' campaigns. The Act was also linked to the movement against the Poll Tax with 1,000 anti-Poll tax unions on estates and suburbs being the largest civil disobedience campaign in British history with 14 million people refusing to pay at some stage. (98)

1990. Council rents increased from an average of £6.20 in 1979 to £23.72 in 1990. (97)

1992. Mass tenant rallies were held against compulsory competitive tendering of housing management. (82)

1996. The '1996 Housing Act' amended the homeless regulations to encourage the use of the courts to grant injunctions against tenants. The Act also introduced the idea of "Local Housing Companies" as a vehicle for transfer and privatization. (96)

1998. "Defend Council Housing" founded, but the fight against council housing privatisation started much earlier. Defend Council housing acted to unite and co-ordinated the opposition against the destruction of council housing. (31)

Governments acts against Council Housing

The picture above of a demonstration on 25th March 2017 by Southwark Defend Council Housing.

By the end of the 1990s. More than two million council houses in Britain had been sold to their tenants under right-to-buy. (67)

2002. Arm's length Management Organisations (ALMOs) were introduce by government. (101)

2004. Building by councils drops to an all-time low of just 130 dwellings across the country. Defend Council Housing managed get a motion supporting council housing passed at the Labour Party conference in 2004. (31)

2006. The amount of housing managed by Registered Social Landlords, including transferred organisations, outnumbers council homes for the first time. (82)

2010. Between 1997-2010 when the Blair and Brown governments were in power for 13 years 2.61 million homes were built a mere 7,870 of them being council houses. (94)

2011. Definition of "affordable housing" introduced. A conservative think-tank set up and chaired by Iain Duncan Smith, conceived the idea of both the term of so called "affordable rent" and right-to-buy for housing association tenants.

Governments acts against Council Housing

2012. The Tory Lib-Dem coalition government doubled the right-to-buy discount to £75,000. The figure went up to £100,000 in London. They falsely pledged they would replace every home sold with a newly built home. At January 20016 only 1 in 9 have been replaced. (91)

2013 The Government announces a horrendous housing benefit cap that was to be phased in. The cuts in housing benefit hit the most disadvantaged groups in society and has led to the increase in homelessness. It was predicted that nationally 936,960 households will lose out, with the average 1-bedroom claimant losing £11 a week. (81)

2015. A Freedom of Information request in September 2015 showed 26 of 33 London councils moved homeless households to other parts of the South East of England. (78)

The Governments DCLG English Housing Survey of 2014-2015 found the private rented sector had the highest proportion of 'non-decent' homes 29% compared with 14 per cent in the social rented sector and 19 per cent of owner-occupied homes. (49)

In May 2015. The BBC radio 4 revealed that "Viability assessments" are used by property developers to prevent councils from "affordable housing". Section 106 agreements are used by councils to reach agreements with developers for supplying so-called affordable housing as part of the plans to build new homes. But "commercial confidentiality" is then used by developers to hide the full scrutiny of their costs. The Growth and Infrastructure Act of April 2013 then allows them to renegotiate and reduce the amount of so-called affordable housing due to a claim made of not being able to make a reasonable profit – a profit typically set at a market level of 20%.

Councils are effectively bribed by developers to concede when "commuted sums" are used to pay councils money by developers. This money is not ring-fenced to housing and due to financial constraints of councils this money is often used for purposes other than providing housing. (121)

Extracts for the London Tenants Federation - Briefing November 2015 - Setting the record straight on subsidy - Putting the record straight

Governments, the media and others consistently make incorrect statements about social housing tenants being 'subsidised'.

Social housing tenants' rents are NOT SUBSIDISED by the public purse. Social rents are cheaper (a lot cheaper in London) than market rents, simply because social housing landlords don't make a profit on them, while private landlords do.

Governments acts against Council Housing

Social rents cover the cost of management, maintenance and repairs of tenants' homes and paying-off the interest on loans taken out by landlords to build the homes in the first place.

Affordable-rent tenants with rents of up to 80% market rents pay for all the above and contribute to the cost of building new affordable rent homes. In fact, they pay twice since they also contribute to this (along with everyone else) through their taxes.

Between 1997 and 2008. Council tenants paid £1.9 billion more in rent (through the redistributive national Housing Revenue Account system) than the government allocated to councils to manage, maintain, carry out major repairs and repay debt on their homes. When councils became 'self-financing', in 2012, they took on the existing council housing debt plus an additional £7.6 billion of national debt (which is serviced through council tenants' rents) on the basis that councils would have a better deal in terms of the future funding of management, maintenance and major repairs to their homes (which had as far back as 2005/6 been assessed, by the Building Research Establishment, as being underfunded).

Homeowners are subsidised through the public purse. Homeowners get capital gains tax relief and pay no tax on the value of their homes (except council tax, which tenants also pay). The combined effects of taxes, like stamp duty and inheritance tax and the various tax reliefs, was a net subsidy in 2013/14 of over £14 billion. A further £723 million was provided in 2012/13 in renovation grants, right-to-buy discounts, support for mortgage interest payments and low-cost homeownership subsidy.

Buy-to-let owners get mortgage tax relief while resident homeowners do not. This has meant that many of them had little or no tax on the rental income they receive. Changes have now been made to ensure their tax relief is only at the basic tax rate of 20% phased in over a four-year period starting in 2017.

The tax relief will fall to 7%, 50% next year, 25% in 2019 and zero in 2020, and will instead be replaced by a 20% tax credit.

The building of social-rented homes (and other types of affordable housing including shared ownership) is subsidised. Current subsidy for affordable housing (for 2015-20) is £4.7 billion nationally (just under £1 billion nationally each year).

If, as argued, it is reverted to subsidising the building of social-rented homes, rather than less subsidy for affordable rents which costs more in the long run, it would be better for tenants and would cost the taxpayer less.

Governments acts against Council Housing

Around a third of London council homes have been sold through right to buy and nationally around 1.89 million homes have been sold since 1980.

Despite the £60 billion or more capital receipts gained from Right-to-Buy (principally by the Government) the majority have not been replaced and are no longer in supply for future tenants. This is despite a commitment from the government that a new home would be built for every additional social-rented home sold.

Private sector housing development in England is subsidised

The total package of financial support from Government for private sector housing investment amounts to more than £30 billion. This includes £518 million in grants, £13.7 billion in loans and £16.5 billion in guarantees. It covers the subsidy for help-to- buy equity schemes and mortgage guarantees, right-to- buy, private rented sector guarantees, built-to-rent, loans for infrastructure to unlock large housing sites, funds to start small housing developments, local growth fund, locally led Garden Cities, housing zones, new homes bonus, 'Getting Britain Building', Custom Build Investment and service plot funds and New Buy guarantee schemes.

Housing benefit

Both private and social housing tenants can claim housing benefit to support them due to housing costs they can't afford. Having insufficient new social-rented homes built has meant that households that might otherwise have been able to afford the cost of social rents are dependent on benefits. This increases the overall benefit bill. Spending on housing benefit has risen by £650 million a year since 2009-10 and is expected to reach £27 billion by 2018/19. Private renters comprise 32% of households claiming housing benefit but the amount claimed by them is 38% of the housing benefit bill. (131)

2016. In May the Housing and Planning Bill was passed. London Mayor Sadiq Khan opposes demolition if not supported by tenants. Yet invents his own version of affordable rents, does very little to prevent demolitions. Government is forced to back down on PAY TO STAY plans. (77)

While council homes are not available to the young generation, private purchase of housing is also not available to most when to do so they will need to have a £64,000 salary to afford the average home by 2020. This is an increase of nearly a fifth on the £52,000 needed for a typical first-time buyer's mortgage in 2016. This is reflected in the drop-in home ownership from 73% in 2003 to 64% in 2016 (85) (105)

Governments acts against Council Housing

The scale of decline of council housing from 2003 to 2017

Year	Owner Occupied	Privately rented	Housing Associations (Renamed "Private Registered Providers")	Social rented Local Authority
2003	14,752,000	2,549,000	1,651,000	2,457,000
2004	14,986,000	2,578,000	1,702,000	2,335,000
2005	15,100,000	2,720,000	1,802,000	2,166,000
2006	15,052,000	2,987,000	1,865,000	2,087,000
2007	15,093,000	3,182,000	1,951,000	1,987,000
2008	15,067,000	3,443,000	2,056,000	1,870,000
2009	14,968,000	3,705,000	2,128,000	1,820,000
2010	14,895,000	3,912,000	2,180,000	1,786,000
2011	14,827,000	4,140,000	2,255,000	1,726,000
2012	14,754,000	4,286,000	2,304,000	1,693,000
2013	14,685,000	4,465,000	2,331,000	1,682,000
2014	14,674,000	4,623,000	2,343,000	1,669,000
2015	14.684,000	4,773,000	2,387,000	1,643,000
2016	14,801,00	4,832.000	2,430,000	1,612,000
2017	15,050,000	4,798,000	2,444.000	1,602,000
2018	15,277.000	4,808,000	2,452,000	1,592,000

Table 2: Dwellings stock in England by tenure as at 31 March 2003 to 2018

Source: Ministry of Housing, Communities & Local Government DCLG Housing Statistics, Table 104, Live Tables on Housing Stock, (100)

Governments acts against Council Housing

The decline of new-build local authority social housing 1953 to 2017

	Privately owned	Housing Association	Local Authorities	All dwellings
1953	64,870	16,800	245,160	326,820
Above line shows that in 1953 Local Authorities built the largest amount of housing				
2008	155,100	31,590	630	187,320
2009	121,500	34,790	840	157,130
2010	105,250	29,380	1,360	135,990
2011	105,450	32,190	3,100	140,710
2012	107,670	31,400	2,510	141,580
2013	106,760	26,750	2,080	135,590
2014	115,060	27,930	2,150	145,140
2015	134,320	34,960	2,730	172,020
2016	138,980	29,090	3,290	171,350
2017	159,220	32,320	3,280	194,830
Average	124,931	31,040	1,156	158,166

Average figures for 3 types of tenure over 10 years
This shows that local authority house building being at an all-time low
communities.gov.uk/publications/review-new-dwelling-starts-and-completions

There was a huge shift in decline of new build Council Housing which had reduced by 32% from 2003 to 2014. At the same time private-rented housing increases by 80% and Housing Association rentals increased by 42% over this period

By 2017, 40% of homes sold under Right to Buy were now in the hands of private landlords. (67)

From April 2019 the Government announced that the Right to Buy discount would increase to £82,800, or £110,500 if you live in London. (91)

History of Southwark Council Housing

In 1899. The Metropolitan Borough of Bermondsey was created and in the 1920's and 30's, became known as 'Red Bermondsey' due to the surge in trade union struggles. The council's aim was to increase the standards of living for thousands of poor people in the borough. Policies aimed at tackling deprivation were assisted by Alfred and Ada Salter, both Councillors and then MP and Mayor respectively. They set about constructing decent quality council blocks and cottage-style dwellings. This was enabled by the slum clearances in Salisbury Street and was built by the council's own workforce DLO. This included the building of a public health centre ('Prevention Is Better Than Cure'), public baths and laundry and one of the first council housing estates – the Wilson Gove estate in Bermondsey. (67) The beginning of the 1900's, saw the Bermondsey Tenants Protection League and the local branch of the Independent Labour Party that added pressure for working-class housing reform.

The three metropolitan boroughs which now make up Southwark and the London County Council (LCC) built more homes after 1945 than in the inter-war period. In the early post-war period, most council housing being built in Southwark was in the form of houses with gardens or low-rise flats.

Above shown a picture of Wilson Grove Estate Bermondsey that was Built by the council DLO and opened in 1928, this was shortly followed up by its DLO building the Spa Road Estate. (68)

History of Southwark Council Housing

In 1927 the Conservatives had intervened to reduce local wages and welfare payments. But despite this, the achievements of 'Red Bermondsey' remained. By 1938, Bermondsey council had built 2,252 dwellings and the London-wide LCC had built another 4,800 homes in Southwark. During the post-war period of 1945-1955, a further 9,600 homes had been built by Bermondsey and the LCC. This had meant the death rate from disease and poverty had dramatically reduced because of the re-housing programme and the visionary health policies that had been put into effect.

1965. The boroughs of Bermondsey, Southwark and Camberwell had been amalgamated to form the London Borough of Southwark. At this time much of Southwark's housing including its social housing had fallen into disrepair.

The 1960s saw the beginning of the construction of the Heygate and Aylesbury Estates, built to house 9,500 people. By the year 2000, both faced the politician's attacks from their vast demolition and regeneration projects.

In the Docklands, in 1971. Southwark and Bermondsey began to see the conversion of warehouses and factories into private residential housing and office developments.

Southwark began to have work carried out to its inter-war estates as early as 1975. This work was mainly carried out by its own housing works division DLO.

Housing owned by the LCC was transferred to Southwark in 1980, bringing the total stock managed by the council at that time to 62,000 units.

In 1981, the Conservative government created the "London Docklands Development Corporation" (LDDC). This acted in opposition to Southwark's own plans. The LDDC aimed to attract private finance for regeneration and was subsidised from public taxes by £1,098 million between 1981 and 1990. Bob Mellish, the then Labour MP for Southwark and Bermondsey, became the vice-chair of the Corporation and ex-Council leader John O'Grady was appointed as another board member.

The docklands "Enterprise Zone" was established in 1982 with a 10-year deal of no rates with investments offset against tax for office and commercial developments and no planning inquiries needed.

In 14 years, 1,600 housing units were completed in the LDDC Bermondsey Riverside area. Of this a staggering 96% were for owner-occupation. This in a London borough that had a rate of council house occupancy at 51% of the resident population in 1991. But local people put up a fight against the developments.

History of Southwark Council Housing

Political activists in the North Southwark area put out flyers, held public meetings and fly-posted against the rampant exploitative speculation and especially opposing the Hay's Wharf and Butler's Wharf developments.

'Five Estates' regeneration continued to reduce Southwark's council housing

The North Peckham estate regeneration, also known as Southwark's Five Estates (i.e. Sumner, North Peckham, Willowbrook, Gloucester Grove and Camden), was approved by Southwark Council in April 1995. At the time this was the biggest single regeneration scheme in the country. The total value was £290 million, which included a £60 million grant from the government. It was completed in 2004 with a net loss of 1,184 of social rented homes. (67)

2000. Southwark Council, and other councils throughout the country, initiated a move aimed at transferring all its housing stock to another social landlord. But despite a large propaganda campaign, they were defeated by a counter-campaign from tenant's groups and "Defend Council Housing".

In 2002 Arm's length Management Organisations (ALMOs) were introduced by government and shortly after the council started to promote the transfer of their housing stock to these organisations or to Housing Associations. Today ALMOs continue to be a threat despite them previously being regularly rejected by Southwark's tenants.

Some recent events of Southwark Council Housing

Southwark Council's rhetoric and what is being delivered on council housing

In October 2012, Southwark commissioned a report into its housing. This was full of the facts about why council housing was far better for the people of Southwark. While initially the council had hypocritically given its full support to this report, it then went in the opposite direction.

On 6th July 2013, The Council met to make its decisions over its housing plans

The council leader reported that: "We want to build more council homes for Southwark's present and future residents as part of the increased housing capacity of all tenures which we need to deliver across our borough". **He said, "We can now conclude with some certainty that not only can we afford to retain our housing stock, but that any stock transfers or significant reduction in the numbers of that stock would not make any financial sense for us as a council." (my emphasis)**

History of Southwark Council Housing

He added: "This report provides a solid evidential basis for us to restate our unequivocal commitment to council housing in our borough, managed for and by our residents and to set about creating an ambitious strategy to build even more new council homes for Southwark and London". (65)

Southwark said in a further statement (2014) its future housing would include:

• 11,000 new council homes by 2043, (1,500 of these by 2018) and hundreds more shared ownership properties

• 20,000 net new homes in the next ten years of which 7,000 will be affordable homes, ensuring these are genuinely affordable to our residents

• Unlocking several housing sites in key locations across Southwark such as Canada Water and Old Kent Road

• Working in partnership to develop good quality, well managed privately owned and rented homes"

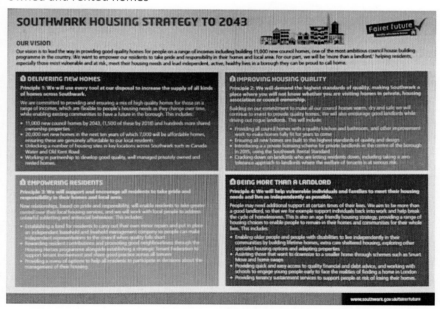

Quality, affordable housing

DM1   Affordable homes

Planning permission will be granted for:

1   A minimum of 35% affordable housing where at least 70% of the affordable housing is for social rent and up to 30% is intermediate where developments provide 10 or more homes, as set out below, unless affordable housing requirements have been set through an area action plan. The affordable housing requirement will be calculated on a per sqm basis of the entire Gross Internal Area of the building used as dwellings:

Table 1: Affordable housing requirements

Market Housing	Affordable housing	
	A minimum of 35%	
Up to 65%	Intermediate housing	Social rented housing
	Up to 10.5%	A minimum of 24.5%

Comment

What stands out in the above statement is the part that pledges "11,000 new council homes by 2043". The question must then be asked again and again: "Could the council be trusted to deliver on providing 11,000 new council homes over what is such a long timescale of 29 years?:

What are the facts - fast forward to 2019?

Southwark is now demolishing and selling off council homes faster than it is building them.

Official statistics from the Government's live tables on local authority dwellings stock show that since the manifesto pledge in 2014 **there has been a net reduction in Southwark's council housing stock of 476 council homes**

Meanwhile, on 30th Oct 2018 Southwark Council Cabinet report confirmed that the council had built just 262 council homes over 5 years.

It was also pointed out that several senior council officers involved in the regenerations have gone on to work for Lendlease, the developer of the Elephant & Castle project. While Council leader Peter John also came under criticism for accepting Olympic tickets from Lendlease and an all-expenses paid trip to Cannes on the French Riviera.

History of Southwark Council Housing

Southwark Councils 'affordable housing' criteria

What the above statement means is that over the next 26 years Southwark plans less than 25% of all housing will be for social rented homes. They are largely abandoning council housing in favour of the individual private-home ownership and privately rented homes.

They intend to go much further with many more demolitions of council housing estates. Estates which contain many thousands of Southwark's existing social housing tenants.

In November 2013, it was revealed that "Lendlease" (the contractor in charge of the demolition and rebuilding of the Heygate estate in the Elephant & Castle) was one of the major construction companies that were sued for their part in the practice of blacklisting of 700 building worker employees who are involved in trade union activities. This news came just a year after Lendlease was fined $56m for defrauding public authorities in New York.

Kim Humphreys, the Council's former Deputy Leader and Cabinet member for Housing responsible for the shameful demolition of the Heygate estate, reappears at the Elephant & Castle as a consultant acting for developer Delancey & Co. Humphreys follows in the footsteps of former Labour Council leader Jeremy Fraser and former Cabinet member for regeneration Steve Lancashire who left the Council to set up a multi-million pound consultancy "Four Communications" which has advised developers on the controversial Eileen House scheme, the King's Reach Tower, 'One Blackfriars', 'Neo-Bankside', Ludgate & Sampson House and The Shard. (June 2014 - Revolving Doors)

In 2015 Southwark announced it will be setting up its own housing company so it can defy government rules and borrow money to build its planned 11,000 new social rented homes over the next 26 years. In the newspaper "Southwark News" on 30th July 2015 it was reported that "Southwark Housing Company Ltd" (SHC) which is a separate limited company, "will not be needed for a few years yet as it is able to work comfortably within the borrowing cap". (72)

The danger now exist that this new "Special Purpose Vehicle" could be used to do away with various existing rights of Southwark tenants. As in the case in Lambeth and other councils for example, where this has led to higher rents. Also, this must not be used to continue with the use of corrupt and discredited contractors, but Instead Southwark should bring back a new-build DLO.

History of Southwark Council Housing

The Aylesbury estate

Southwark's Aylesbury estate was the largest social housing estate in Europe. It was home to 7,500 residents, the size of a small town. For years, this estate was vilified by the media as a den of crime and poverty. This stood in complete contrast to what the tenants on this estate felt, as for many years' they had fought against its privatisation, including holding a ballot in 2001 with a 70% turn out and a 73% majority to remain as Southwark Council tenants. Yet the Council was determined to have its way and went on to instruct consultants Capita to develop a "manifesto for change" and a "renewal strategy" that culminated in 2005 with the council deciding for the demolition and redevelopment of the area.

The Aylesbury estate residents campaigned to stay where they were and said:

- The scheme failed to ensure that social rented housing will be provided that was viable and deliverable.

- There are other cheaper options than demolition.

- Refurbishment was not properly considered when the decision to demolish the estate was taken.

- The scheme will not promote the social well-being of the area.

- The CPO breaches the human rights of the various resident leaseholders.

On 7th April 2014, the Council announced it had awarded a contract for the development of the estate to the Notting Hill Housing Trust (NHH). This was the beginning of what could be the privatisation of what is a large part of the council's services. Services currently run by council's employees that now face the threat of being outsourced.

Notting Hill's CEO, Kate Davies, was once on the far left of politics but in my opinion is now helping to drive up the cost of rents and privatisation of housing. She was a fellow of the Centre for Social Justice, a conservative think-tank set up and chaired by Iain Duncan Smith, which conceived the idea of both "affordable rent" and right-to-buy for housing association tenants. (Notting Hill Housing Association merged with Genesis Housing Association in April 2018).

Secretary of State knocks back the plans for Aylesbury's demolition

In September 2016, the Secretary of State for Communities and Local Government, Sajid Javid, rejected the compulsory purchase order (CPO) of eight leaseholder's flats on the Aylesbury Estate. On 19th December 2016 Southwark's appeal to knock down the Aylesbury homes is rejected a second time

History of Southwark Council Housing

In November 2018, the Tory housing secretary, James Brokenshire, confirmed Southwark's application for a compulsory purchase order (CPO) on the estate.

While disappointed over this decision after such a lengthy battle being waged by the leaseholders, the construction work is a long way from completion, and campaigners vow to continue the fight for council social housing.

A previously unseen document dated from 2014 was leaked to the Guardian newspaper in September 2018, this showed that Southwark Council had assumed all the financial risk involved in its regeneration project of the Aylesbury estate while at the same time a return to the housing association redeveloping the estate was guaranteed. (117)

Southwark's Ledbury estate tower blocks - threat of collapse

On August 10th 2017, after denials of major safety problems on the Ledbury estate, Southwark admitted that huge refurbishment works would be needed to ensure it will be safe. The council discovered that works ordered to estates in England following the deadly Ronan Point tower block collapse in 1968 may not have been carried out on the Ledbury. This has raised the many fire safety issues which have occurred since the aftermath of the Grenfell fire.

In October 2018 the council decided that the Ledbury estate's tower blocks could be safely refurbished and not demolished. The cost would be partly met by building new homes on land next door. The Council said that "at least half of these new homes will be council homes". (It should have been all of them – author) (115)

Southwark's council homes continue to decline

In April 2019 Southwark agreed a huge redevelopment scheme in an area of the Old Kent Road that is surrounded with existing council housing. Yet this new development will only have 237 social rental homes out of a planned 1,113 new homes. (108)

The 35% Campaign

The 35% Campaign based in Southwark grew out of the fight against Southwark Council's actions in the demolition of the Heygate estate. Their most recent battle has been over the Elephant & Castle shopping centre.

HEYGATE ESTATE
HOMES DESTROYED: 1,034
HOMES BUILT: 2,704
AT SOCIAL RENT: 82
'REGENERATION'
BROUGHT TO YOU BY Southwark Council

35% website graph (71)

Elephant & Castle Shopping Centre - latest for-profit-seeking Delancey & Co

In 2017, it was revealed that 979 new homes would be built at the Elephant & Castle Shopping Centre, but not at social rents and with no room for current shopkeepers.

Yet Southwark's policy for the Elephant & Castle required a minimum of 35% affordable housing, of which 50% should be social rental. The developer is an offshore company registered in the BVI and Bermuda.

Since then there have been many struggles by those adversely affected by these proposals. On 5th March 2019 a coalition of local people and groups fighting for a fairer regeneration at the Elephant & Castle, including the 35% Campaign, supported a legal application to overturn the planning approval for the redevelopment of the Elephant & Castle. (71)

Southwark Council's links to the development industry

The 35% Campaign also reported on the work of the journalist Anna Minton who found that "20% of Southwark's 63 councillors work as lobbyists" for developers in the planning industry and that a significant number of Councillors and Council officers are making use of a "well-oiled revolving door" to the industry. (71)

Campaign to 'Kill the Housing Act'

The campaign to defeat the threat from the Housing Bill was one of our most important events. If we had not rescinded some of the most crucial parts of this Act it could have marked the end of social housing as we know it.

Campaign to 'Kill the Housing Act

THE HOUSING AND PLANNING ACT 2016 – KEY MEASURES

- Lifetime secure tenancies would end as council tenancies will only be allowed for two to five years with no right to pass it on to children.

- Means-testing being introduced, with landlords having access to a tenant's personal income information, and if households start to earn over £40,000 in London, £30,000 outside London (a couple on the living wage) they will be hit with a PAY-TO-STAY TAX for the difference between their social rent and the market rent. In April 2016 the government backed down from making PAY-TO-STAY compulsory on local authorities, but it still allowed them to introduce it locally.

- Local authorities forced to sell "high value" properties whenever they come vacant (what flat in London is not high value?)

- Housing association tenants will get the right to buy, so reducing stock further.

- Cost associated by this right to buy will come from the forced sale (the robbery) of councils' housing.

Government forced to back on many changes of 2016 Housing and Planning Act (extracts from House of Commons Library briefing, 27 September 2018)

Summary

It is now over 3 years since the Housing Bill was given Royal Assent on 12 May 2016. Some of the Act's key provisions are yet to be implemented. The Government confirmed that several measures would not be implemented.

- Measures aimed at tackling "rogue" landlords and agents came into force in April 2018.

- The mandatory "pay to stay" policy has been dropped.

- The requirement on local authorities to offer only fixed-term tenancies has also been dropped.

- The Act does not give assured housing association tenants a statutory right-to-buy their homes.

- The Government has said that they "will not bring the Higher Value Assets provisions of the Housing and Planning Act 2016 into effect".

Regulations aimed at reducing the regulation of Housing Associations came into force on 16 November 2017. (47)

Housing Associations

Governments expand Housing Associations while running down Council Housing

Housing Associations were one of the first providers of social housing. There original declared purpose was very similar to that of council-housing providers: "non-profit making organisations that provide low-cost social housing". Any trading surplus to be used to "maintain existing housing and help finance new homes".

All this has changed as the government has made it clear they have moved them away from being just providers of social rental housing: Their new name is "Private Registered Providers" (PRPs).

The background to this was the Housing Acts of 1985 and 1988 which had facilitated the transfer of council housing to Housing Associations.

The 1988 Act redefined the associations as non-public bodies, permitting access to private finance, which was a strong motivation for transfer as public sector borrowing was severely constrained. (120)

Housing Associations controlled 36.5% of all the UKs social housing by 2003 and by 2016 it controlled over 60%. (99)

Housing Association tenants marginalised

After the election of Margaret Thatcher in 1980, the large-scale so-called 'voluntary' transfer of council-housing stock to Housing Associations was used to diminish the amount of council housing. These transfers hugely increased after the election of Tony Blair in 1997 and HAs have become less socially motivated and more and more profit driven. Such changes include the increase in salaries paid to their top officials with hundreds of very well-paid chief executives.

Today Housing Associations generally operate with fewer rights for tenants than council housing. As long ago as January 1989, if you became a Housing Association tenant, the grounds for possession of your property were based on you being an "assured private tenant". You then would have fewer rights than a "protected tenant" whose landlord could only repossess your accommodation in very limited and specified circumstances and you also had greater rights over your landlords putting up rents. If you became a Housing Association tenant with a "starter tenancy" or became a "demoted tenant" you also would have fewer rights.

Housing associations

1. Governments fear the democratic process of electing political parties that control council housing and with it any possible political opposition that may arise. They don't like any rebellions against their authority, rebellions that are successful in challenging their control.

2. Do not forget the history of rent strikes, poll tax and rate-capping rebellions, struggles against attacks on social housing.

3. Unlike council social housing, elected political parties don't have any control of Housing Associations. They are in the main controlled by management committees comprised of all sorts of unelected people from private business, the churches and others.

4. Housing Associations employ very few if any directly employed construction workers to build and maintain their properties but instead enable private construction contractors to take control of the work.

   This contrasts with many councils who have trade union-organised building DLOs which are starting to expand or starting new ones.

We need Housing Associations as social rent tenants

We must work with the tenants' organisation of Housing Associations to reverse all the adverse cuts made to them. And with their agreement they should be given the right to have their homes transferred to councils and become part of the councils' social-housing properties.

TMOs and ALMOs

All outsourcing of council housing must end, whether this is to: Housing Associations, Tenant Management Organisations (TMO) and Arm's Length Management Organisations (ALMO).

TMOs and ALMOs, are much more of a direct route for transfers of council housing to Housing Associations or being sold. All this fragmentation of course leads to the break-up of what are council services, its various housing employees, including its building DLO workers.

The Grenfell Tower Disaster

The fire that took place on the 14th June 2017 at the Grenfell Tower block in Kensington & Chelsea claiming the lives of 71 people, with many others having horrendous injuries and being subjected to toxic materials, must never be forgotten and never happen again. The best way to do that is to make sure we reverse all the attacks made against our housing.

The repercussions resulting from this fire are huge, they expose the double standards between what on the one hand is an extremely rich borough that exists alongside what is a very poor community that is not listened to and is subjected to less safety protection from fires. It also shows the effect from the many years of governments dismantling services that protect us and the deregulation of health and safety law.

Many false promises for a proper public inquiry were made to those affected. This continued when on December 2018 it was announced that the outcome from the investigations would have to wait at least two years before any criminal charges could be brought as the Police were unlikely to submit a file to the Crown Prosecution Service before late 2021.

The Grenfell Tower Disaster

Also the inquiry chair, Sir Martin Moore-Bick, had not yet confirmed a date or venue for the second stage of hearings, which will examine the causes of the disaster. (70)

An outcry followed when it was discovered in May 2019 that Sacha Jevans, who was the executive director of Kensington & Chelsea Tenant Management Organisation (KCTMO), which managed the building and oversaw the £10m recladding works, had been invited to lecture on ways to "improve risk management and building safety post-Grenfell" at the Chartered Institute of Housing conference in Manchester in June. (69)

Some key developments from 2017 onwards

2017 General Election – Tories win but rely on DUP for a majority vote – Corbyn's left-wing leadership brings increase in Labour vote

8th June 2017: This was a day that saw a historical shift towards progressive socialist politics in Britain that could give us a greater opportunity to reverse the decline in council housing.

While the Tories won the most seats they were trapped in a hung parliament. This led to them giving the Northern Ireland's right-wing DUP a political bribe so they could count on their vote to give them a majority.

Jeremy Corbyn had led his party to top 40% of the vote - just shy of the share it won in 2001 under Tony Blair. Equally this was a huge setback towards those 80% of Labour MPs who continue to oppose Corbyn, as well as most of the Labour councillors who were continuing to implement Tory policies in their localities.

A turning point came in the election when Teresa May had to backtrack on her announced election programme that included placing a limit on the universal benefit of the winter fuel allowance to pensioners and taking the value of people's homes into account in the means test for social care at home (known as the dementia tax).

Other UK party politicians collaborate in the Government's destruction of social housing

Assurances were given in the run-up to the election of Sadiq Khan as the Mayor of London in 2016, that demolition of social housing should only be permitted where it does not result in any loss of social housing.

Yet ever since many estates have been demolished and the vast majority have been replaced by private homes rented at so called "affordable rents".

Some key developments from 2017 onwards

These affordable homes are based on one-third of average local household incomes, of between £35,000 and £45,000 a year. Yet in London annual household earnings could be as wide as £25,000 to £60,000, depending on the area of London. Also, long-term tenancies are abandoned as the tenure period is only for up to five years. These so called "affordable rents" are around 67% of market rents. The big difference is that London Living Rents will be much more affordable to the middle-income households they are aimed at, rather than to those from low-income households. (114)

So, what does this mean for Southwark and for those in many other similar areas in our country?

Below I have used a chart which shows the income bands in Southwark as an example to what are very similar to many other councils to demonstrate why we just cannot afford the housing policies that are being pursued by all three main political parties.

Total Southwark gross household income by bands

Income bands	South East London and Lambeth	Southwark
Under £5,200	3%	5%
£5,200 - £10,400	10%	14%
£10,401 - £15,600	16%	25%
£15,601 - £20,800	15%	21%
£20,801 - £26,000	9%	8%
£26,001 - £31,200	15%	8%
£31,201 - £36,400	9%	8%
£36,401 - £41,600	6%	4%
£41,601 -£46,800	4%	3%
Over £46,800	8%	5%

Source: Cobweb Private Rented Sector Study 2014 – Borough Summary (116)

Many other reasons exist as to why we must oppose the London Mayor's housing affordability criteria. For example:

- For those living in London there were 820,000 low-paid jobs in 2018 – at least 1 in 5 jobs in London were low paid. (75)

Some key developments from 2017 onwards

- The "Employment Support Allowance" (this is an allowance for those with disabilities who are unemployed) was cut from £102 a week to £73 a week if you are age 25 and over as from April 2017. (74)

- Because private landlords can choose who they want as tenants they don't have to rent to those on housing benefit. That is why we need more not fewer homes being based on the less costly council social home rent criteria.

- A huge 500% increase between 2011 to 2016 of those who work on the precarious work of zero-hour contracts in London are unable to afford so-called "affordable rents". (73)

Pensioners and Housing

More than 2 million older people are suffering physical and mental ill-health and are facing early death because of living in substandard and non-accessible homes according to a report made in July 2019 by the cross-party group of MPs involved with ageing and older people

The report says sub-standard housing is costing the NHS £1.4bn every year. The report also predicts that the number of older people renting in the private sector, often in unsafe, unsuitable and unhealthy accommodation, is set to soar in the coming years. (129)

There is so much publicity out there from those who are attempting to blame older people for the housing crisis. Yet the facts are fewer than 48% of 55-64-year-olds own their property outright. An estimated 2.6 million older people, who have assets greater than £100,000, survive on an income of less than £15,000 a year and just 2% of housing stock is constructed with pensioners in mind. (119)

With hardly any opposition from our MPs, some of our poorest pensioner couples have now lost up to £7,000 a year due to changes made to pensioners' housing credits in May 2019. This means couples where only one partner is over the state pension age (now 65, or up to 68 for both men and women depending on when they were born) will no longer receive the extra benefit.

Housing will become more and more unaffordable if other attacks being planned on pensioners are not stopped.

The House of Lords' report of Intergenerational Fairness recommendations published on 25th April 2019 followed those from a similar report made by a select committee of MPs.

Some key developments from 2017 onwards

The focus of these reports is to turn back the clock on pensioners' universal benefits such as: Removal of the triple lock State Pension.

Phasing out free TV licences based on age, a five-year limit for receipt of free bus passes and Winter Fuel Payments, treating them as part of taxable income.

They are also gearing up to make pensioners pay more for social care. We must insist that the funding for pensioners' universal benefits must continue to be met from general taxation - with the higher paid having to pay more.

The first moves to implement their plans came when the BBC announced it intended to means-test the over 75s' TV licence from June next year. Pensioners re-acted angrily when "National Pensioners Convention" (NPC) groups across the UK staged over 20 demos outside local BBC offices, involving around 1,000 people. In London. Campaigners also stopped the traffic in Oxford Circus. At the same time a petition launched by Age UK and backed by the NPC reached nearly 600,000.

These unprecedented attacks require that all pensioners, whether today's or our future ones, must now be prepared to start a huge campaign to prevent these cuts from taking place.

Haringey social housing scandal

In February 2017, campaign groups protested at the Haringey Development Vehicle, Haringey council's proposal for a two billion-pound joint venture housing deal with the developer Lendlease. Residents, unions and Labour Party members condemned the plans as a 'social cleansing programme' that would result in thousands of council house tenants being removed from their homes with no guarantee of return.

In July 2018 there were newly elected councillors in Haringey who then voted to halt the Lendlease deal. This after many of the Labour councillors who backed the joint venture had either stood down or had been deselected by party members. Former council leader Claire Kober also stepped down and then went on to join a regeneration and housing management company.

Unfortunately, after this victory the Council continued to accommodate Lendlease at a 2,500-home exclusive development in North Tottenham, although in Summer 2018 the GLA stepped in to insist on a residents' ballot, which could scupper the scheme.

Some key developments from 2017 onwards

In December 2018, Haringey agreed a housing development at Tottenham Hale on 60% council-owned land, with 131 new council rent homes and another 899 homes deemed "unaffordable", which campaigners said could push up house prices and rents in the local area, fuelling gentrification and breaking up local communities. (123)

Cressingham Gardens Estate

Since Lambeth Council in 2012 proposed the demolition of Cressingham Gardens' residents and supporters have campaigned tirelessly to save what is mainly a social housing estate. Residents went on to present their own scheme and won a judicial review that stated the council acted unlawfully by removing refurbishment options from the consultation. With the help of technical experts, residents developed and submitted an alternative plan called "The People's Plan". Only one day after its submission Lambeth Council dismissed the plan and reverted to their decision to demolish the estate.

All the indications are that the threat of demolition is not immediate but could happen anytime over the next five years.

In the meantime Lambeth continues to neglect the estate, allowing it to be run down and unfortunately pushing residents into a position where they have now established a "TMO" and decided to apply for a "Right to manage" status; this they hope will allow the estate to be transferred into the hands of a community trust. Meanwhile, like many London councils, Lambeth continues with the privatisation of its council housing.

Some key developments from 2017 onwards

What is more important to Lambeth and these councils is not their tenants, and neither is it the ownership of the estates that concerns them, it's the valuable land available after demolition that is important to them.

Despite the central demand of the residents: "no demolition without permission", at the time of writing this book in 2019, Lambeth Council continues with its plan to demolish this estate and others in Lambeth.

Housing Benefit for 18-21 year-olds restored after axed 12 months earlier

A successful campaign led to the axing of the decision to end housing benefit for jobless under-22-year-olds. This cruel policy had put over 9,000 young people at risk of homelessness according to homeless organisations.

Above is a picture from the protest in Parliament Square held on 1st April 2017 against axing housing benefits for 18 -21-year olds. The large placard reads: "18-21 RESIST"

Some key developments from 2017 onwards

Homelessness

The Local Government Association (LGA) warned on 23rd March 2019 that there was a 70% rise in temporary accommodation since 2010. Its survey revealed that councils have struggled to cope with the rising numbers of people facing homelessness due to lack of affordable housing.

Since 2017, local authorities have housed more than 200,000 people in temporary accommodation costing a whopping £2million a day, with over half of them children. The number of flats and houses available has plunged to a 24-year low because of the Tories' disastrous right-to-buy policy. (84)

The government's no-fault eviction announcement

2019. In April the government announced it intended to do away with "no fault evictions" (section 21 notices).

This announcement came after evidence was provided by Citizens Advice which showed that in a survey of 2,001 private renters who had made a formal complaint to landlords that within six months of the complaint 46% of them had been evicted. (118)

While this proposal to do away with no-fought evictions is welcome, it is subject to a consultation process and could change and be diluted. So, we need to keep up the pressure and be vigilant until we see the final detail.

This good news is cautioned by the Government's announcement that it will give extra powers to landlords to seek possession when they want to sell their properties or move into it themselves.

Rogue landlords allowed to break the law

It was revealed 2019 in a Freedom of Information Act claim that not a single rogue landlord has been issued with one of the new banning orders, a year after the key new power was introduced in April 2018. It was estimated there were 10,500 rogue landlords operating in England, and that it expected more than 600 of the worst offenders to be entered onto the database. What little progressive changes that have taken place on housing means nothing if they are not enforced. (106)

Those from richer backgrounds are benefiting from home-ownership grants

It was reported in August 2019 that rich households rather than poor ones are benefiting from a £25 billion public subsidy supposedly designed towards helping those from poorer backgrounds to achieve home ownership.

Some key developments from 2017 onwards

More than 5,500 households with an annual income of over £80,000 have been given help with "buy loans schemes" in the past year compared with 4,142 households earning less than £30,000, the Government's own figures have revealed. (132)

Conclusions

The housing crisis is a man-made crisis led by a minority driven by nothing but greed. It's up to us, the majority, to resolve this. The wicked ownership culture in housing, whether it be by individuals or private companies that uses housing to exploit others, must be put to an end.

The housing crisis: what can we learn from history?

Rent controls had been maintained in the UK all the way from the First World War to 1977, when they were consolidated in the Fair Rent Act. This meant that landlords could only increase rents every two years, and only do so if rents of similar properties were increased. This enabled the cost of all forms of housing to be much lower than it is today. The 1977 Fair Rent Act was repealed in 1980 which then allowed rents to continually increase. Added to this has been the continuing increase in the price of land and the building contractors' price fixing activities. This has led to housing costs rising from around 17% of household income in 1983 to 50% today and led to a fifth of the population now living on incomes below the poverty line. All of this has been driven by the policies of successive governments since 1980. (63) (85)

Money given to housing private sector by Government

A huge amount of taxpayer's money is being handed by the government to prop up the private housing sector. Largest amounts going to the property speculators and developers. All this keeps rents high. Government gives subsidies, guarantees/underwrites and provides grants amounting to many £billions each year. This includes:

- Homeowners capital gains tax relief. (60)

- Renovation grants. (59)

- Support for mortgage interest payments. (58)

- Low cost homeownership subsidy. (60)

- Right-to-buy has seen around 2.5 million homes being sold since 1980. Despite the £60 billion or more capital receipts gained from RTB (principally by the Government) most of these homes have not been replaced. (61)

Conclusions

- The housing benefit bill has risen from £5 billion in 1989 to £25 billion in 2018. (57)
- The banks and large landlords are making huge profits from the housing crisis. Many of their risks are also being covered by the taxpayer because over £16 billion of underwriting guarantees that are being given to them by the Government. (50)

Residence from all types of housing lose out

Housing insecurity has taken hold for most of the population in the UK both for private and those seeking to rent in the public sector. Many are driven to try and buy their own homes because of costly private-sector rents, or because of a lack of council homes, then face having to pay huge mortgage repayments. Even for those who own their own homes outright, when family relationships break down the high cost of housing then becomes a major factor that forces unwilling partners to continue to live together or leave and then face very limited housing prospects with many becoming homeless. So, we all lose because of not having good regulations that are aimed at providing low-cost good quality housing in our country.

Land ownership and the hoarding of land

The main reason why increased prices of homes are way above what they should be is because of the ever-increasing price of land when in some parts of our country land represents the largest part of providing for new build homes.

The price of land is being deliberately driven up in the UK. This is shown by the fact that in the 20 years between 1983 to 2003 land in Britain had gone up in value more than 16 times. By 2013, private builders had secured planning permission on enough land to build 400,000 homes in England, but not one of those homes had been built. The largest home builders and speculative investment companies deliberately hoard land for which planning permission to build homes has already been given. They wait until it rises in value, then homes that are built command higher prices.

The result being land ownership and property development is now a multi-billion-pound global industry that represented a 51% bubble of the UK's net worth in 2016, higher than any other G7 country. (35)

Yet most of the big landowners benefit from substantial tax breaks at public expense and are based overseas with offshore-registered companies having bought a staggering £170 billion worth of land in England and Wales between 2005 and 2014. (109).

Conclusions

Changes in land tax laws are needed and should include the hoarding of land to be made illegal – in order to lower the cost of land used for housing.

Those on private or social rents and those who own their home and use it as their own sole residency should not be penalised as a result of any new land tax system.

Empty Homes

It is also wrong to hoard homes, especially when left unused while so many are unable to afford housing. Leaving homes vacant just to see it grow in value so as make huge sums of money is morally wrong especially with so many homeless. In 2018 there were 605,891 vacant dwellings in England. While long-term vacant dwellings numbered 205,293. (110)

There are also too many large homes with unoccupied bedrooms. I am not referring to those homes relating to the many working-class families in council housing who may have a real need for a spare bedroom that are wrongly penalised by the government's bedroom tax. What I am saying is that there are many hundreds of thousands of privately-owned homes that don't just have one spare bedroom but have several extra rooms which are not used. It's this sheer extravagant culture of huge homes with several large rooms, 10 or many more rooms, which are occupied by so few people that not only wastes bedrooms but are also a waste of land, energy and other resources. (79)

Demolition verses modernisation

One of biggest scandals in our lifetime is the many council homes that have already been demolished after only having a 20-40 lifespan and those which continue under threat of demolition. The reasons for this are property speculators wanting to get hold of what is greatly valued land then drive up the costs of housing. It's the British version of a Wild West land grab.

To do this the politicians and property speculators peddle a Big Lie by saying:

"Older council homes are outdated and must be demolished and replaced by newer properties". Yes, some do, but most don't and only need being updated and properly maintained. The reverse is the case with private properties when millions of them benefiting from repairs and modernisation. You can see large numbers of private properties built even up to 200 years ago which have not been demolished but have been modernised.

Conclusions

Many of those include those 2.5 million council properties sold under the Right-to-Buy, including those Victorian and Georgian houses which are seen in most cities being greatly valued and expected to have many more years of valid use before they will need to be demolished.

Maximum unity needed across all housing tenures

We must aim for maximum unity among all workers whether they are Council Housing, Housing Association, or private renting tenants or homeowners.

We are all effected by the housing crisis. Most of us have never been given a choice as to whether we wanted to become council tenants, as there was never enough council housing available to be given that choice.

For those so-called asset-rich "baby boomers" born after the Second World War between 1940 and 1960 who became mortgage-paying homeowners, even for those whose sole purpose is a home for their own use, their move can become a huge liability when having to be subjected to various costs. In addition to the moving cost, In London, stamp duty land tax can amount to having to find on average anything between £20,000 to £40,000 for a three-bed home.

3.3 million co-habiting couple families were the fastest growing family type between 1996 and 2016, when they more than doubled from 1.5 million families to 3.3 million families. Yet because they choose not to marry, but jointly own a property, they face tax discrimination if one of them should die. The remaining person will face a 40% tax bill for any property valued above £325,000.

For example, an average 2-4 bed property priced between £600,000-£800,000 in London would carry a tax bill of between £110,00 - £190,000. Most working-class families could not afford these huge sums and those from the family who are left behind can lose the home and be evicted.

For young couples starting out wanting to have kids who have struggled to pay a mortgage after escaping from having to endure paying high private rents, they will typically have a one-bedroom flat or share a home with others.

But to move to having a property that can accommodate the one or two extra bedrooms needed for the children will be impossible without them having to raise enormous sums of money.

Conclusions

Even more so today, for those who succeed in getting a mortgage, the majority will then struggle to be able to pay it because of huge property prices, then to be described as home owners by the media and Governments is far-fetched, when the harsh reality is they will face many years of paying a mortgage before they will own their homes, with increasing numbers of them falling into arrears and facing evictions. Added to this will be many who have student debt of tens of thousands of pounds, then this becomes a lifetime of being shackled to the moneylenders.

We must learn from history

Council housing could have been built far better, far cheaper had we had a majority leadership in our trades unions and in our political parties who were dedicated to serving the people rather than themselves. The drive for council housing was not because of our politicians or many of our trades union leaders. It was forced on them at two major points in our history:

1. The state feared the spread of the rebellion to British workers who, after the First World War, were inspired by the 1917 Russian Revolution and its demands for world revolution to establish genuine worker socialist governments.

2. Secondly workers were not prepared to go back to the conditions of the Great Depression years of the 1930s after having to fight for their country. Those conditions had been generated by the banks and other capitalist financial institutions. Workers then demanded a much better existence and were prepared to fight for it. They demanded and got it and from 1947 onwards council housing began to be more affordable, it was far better housing than that had previously existed when workers were faced with appalling slum housing conditions. "Use of housing to exploit must end and be replaced by housing owned and controlled by all".

The Housing Crisis

What's needed to resolve the Housing Crisis

We must recognise the historic failure of Local and National government to deliver the housing needs for the people of our country. This is because of the emphasis on privatisation of housing that has taken place over the last 50 years. We must see a complete reversal in favour of building public social housing by councils, as the private sector has proven to be incapable of delivering the housing we require.

The housing crisis is not simply due to its lack of supply. It's because of the lack of supply of "TRULY AFFORDABLE HOUSING". Housing is available to all if you are prepared to pay the asking price for it but the price for housing is now, more than ever before, totally out of reach and out of all proportion to its true costs. The price of housing has been driven up by Government's failure to deliver an adequate supply of truly affordable housing from the private sector while at the same time having starved local authorities from providing new social housing and being able to sufficiently maintain existing housing stock.

Governments have reduced social housing by both de-regulation and its use of the Right-to-Buy facilitated by transfer to Housing Associations, Arm's Length Management Organizations (ALMOs), Tenant led Management Organizations (TMOs) and Housing Action Trusts (HATs)

Government cutbacks to building regulations, building inspectors, health and safety regulations did, as was predicted, lead to the tragedy of the Grenfell fire disaster. A totally unnecessary event which saw the loss of 71 people's lives with hundreds of others suffering both physical and mental health injuries as well as the loss of their homes. Disasters that will occur again and again if the housing policies being pursued by Local and National government are not reversed. In terms of financial cost to our people, official figures show that the cost of housing has gone up by nearly 3 times, in real terms, since about 1960.

This has created vast fortunes for construction companies, property developers and landlords. This greed was on display in December 2017 when it was accurately reported that the chief executive of the housebuilding firm Persimmon was awarded a £110m bonus, the highest bonus on record for a listed company, while his 150 most senior staff were between them given more than £500m in bonuses. Due to public outcry the chief executive later reduced his bonus to £75m but then asked to leave. Workers when sacked don't receive any bonus, but it seems you do, and with millions, if you are a chief executive.

What's needed to resolve the Housing Crisis

Yet again it was revealed in February 2019 that Persimmon posted a record profit of £1billion. This, while at the same time the company continued to benefit from the taxpayer-backed Help-to-Buy scheme.

In January 2018 the second largest construction company in the UK, Carillion collapsed with debts of over £1bn and a £600m pension deficit, all left to be picked up by the taxpayer.

At the time of writing this book in October 2019 it has been nearly 2 years since the collapse of, Carillion in January 2018 Yet no action has been taken against the company's directors or senior managers responsible for its collapse. This despite several regulators launching investigations into the circumstances of the company's collapse, including into its financial reporting and whether there was any criminal wrongdoing by Carillion's directors prior to the company's collapse.

At the same time Carillion's two flagship hospital projects the Royal Liverpool hospital and the Midland Metropolitan hospital are years behind schedule with work not yet restarted or only just getting underway.

Unite are taking workers who lost their jobs following Carillion's collapse to an industrial tribunal. Yet the tribunal system forces these workers to have to wait until late 2020 before they can be heard. Unite assistant general secretary Gail Cartmail said:

"The guilty directors and senior managers remain unpunished and are free to pursue new lucrative roles while the innocent workers have a long battle ahead of them in their battle to secure compensation in the courts. Flagship hospital projects are years away from being completed, meanwhile patients and staff have been left to struggle on in facilities that are no longer fit for purpose. Government ministers have clearly washed their hands of the whole mess and now pretend it is no longer their problem. It is quite clear that their needs to be a root and branch reform of company law to prevent similar collapses in the future and the creation of effective regulators with real teeth who are able and willing to tackle bandit capitalism." (134)

A report by the National Audit office in January 2018 said that PFI-funded projects were between 40% to 70% more costly to build than if they were financed by government borrowing. What more do we need to be told to show that the private sector of the construction industry does not work in favour of our interests? This appalling situation must not be allowed to continue.

What's needed to resolve the Housing Crisis

Yet again in March 2019 we saw another major government funded contractor "Interserve", which employed 45,000 workers, collapse. Interserve was working on £2 billion of government contracts, £660 million of them handed out despite profit warnings and debts approaching £700m that showed the firm was in trouble. (34)

Our demands

The only way that the UK housing crisis can be resolved is to take housing out of the so-called free market. We must separate housing from wealth. We can move in this direction by bringing in laws that will:

1. Put a price cap on the purchases of Houses and Housing for rent to allow for truly affordable home ownership and truly affordable rents.

2. End the right-to-buy of all council and Housing Association housing.

3. Increase taxation where there is an accumulation of housing that has many spare rooms without there being any good reason and which are not being used.

4. Changes in land tax laws must be introduced and include provisions for the hoarding of land to be made illegal, and to lower the cost of land used for housing of those on private or social rents and those who own their home and use it as their own sole residency.

5. Set up a national publicly owned construction company that will carry out a massive programme of house-building, house renovations and maintenance. Local authorities will add to this new-build programme by the setting up of new-build Direct Labour Organisations where they do not already exist and to expand them where they do. They will be given the necessary resources to allow them to carry out this task.

6. All restrictions on Building Direct Labour Organisations to be removed.

7. Tenants must be central to the planning and design for new and modernised housing. There should be no return to the top-down approach. House building and house maintenance must meet high standards for: quality, the environment, of being built to last for many years. There must be an adequate supply of homes that are designed to meet the needs of those who are vulnerable and older citizens.

8. All subsidies given by the government to prop up the private housing building sector for the supply of privately owned homes to end.

9. The 2004 Housing Act requirement that allowed private properties to be left vacant only for up to 6 months must be reinstated.

What's needed to resolve the Housing Crisis

10. The scandal of the demolition of thousands of council homes that brings about a waste of materials and human labour must end and be replaced with a policy that whenever possible council housing will be refurbished and maintained to a much higher standard.

11. The Government's current 2016 Housing Act must be abolished in full and be replaced with legislation that restores the right of having a fully secured tenancy and actions taken against exploitative landlords

12. Discrimination against the right of youth to council housing must end.

13. The discrimination over tax on the homes of millions of UK couples who choose not to marry must end.

14. The bedroom tax policy of the government be abolished.

15. Give tenants of "Housing Associations", "Tenant Management Organisations", "Arm's Length Management Organisations" the right to be transferred to councils and for their homes to become part of councils' social housing properties.

16. The misleading name of "affordable housing" at a cost of up to 80% of the housing market cost, that is used to reduce the numbers of much lower-cost social rented homes, must be scrapped.

17. Allow councils to be funded by central government to take over homes of private homeowners who have defaulted on mortgage payments to give them the option to stay in their home as council tenants.

18. Establish legislation so that all existing and new social housing will only be allowed for the sole purpose for accommodation of tenants and not to be used for sale or sub-letting for rent to make a profit. Making a profit from social housing rents to be excluded as any surplus must be ploughed back into expanding and improving to social rental housing stock.

19. A council social housing new-build programme of 300,000 homes each year be established by the Government. This can be achieved as we built even more homes in the 1950s when our country was far less wealthy than we are today.

20. No demolition of council homes be allowed without first those effected being allowed a vote to decide on any proposal.

21. Have a moratorium on all new regeneration schemes and review those schemes currently underway. Only those meeting the applicable criteria listed in the above demands should be allowed to continue.

The growing movement to bring back Council Housing

Reports shows councils bringing services back in house

A report by the Association for Public Service Excellence (APSE) published in May 2019 showed that at least 220 local government contracts had been brought back into council control and that 77% of councils in the UK were now planning to bring services back in-house. (124)

Glasgow City council brings its construction work back in-house

It now has:

- A large new-build, repairs and maintenance section with a workforce of 2,200 all directly employed.
- A manufacturing arm employing 270 workers, 60% of them with disabilities.
- 250 apprentices with 80% re-employed after time served.
- All homes built by the directly employed workforce is social housing owned by Glasgow City council.
- Homes built with high levels of insulation, efficient heating systems with thermal and solar panels.
- Homes that have two-thirds less in energy costs compared to a typical 3-bedroom house. (125)

Liverpool to begin building new council houses for first time in 30 years

On 21st June 2019 Liverpool council announced a target of 10,000 new homes after the Government confirmed a £735m debt over its previous transfer of properties to Housing Associations would be wiped out. However, it has yet to say how many of these homes will be council homes. (127)

Wales builds council houses for the first time in decades

In was reported in May 2019 that Cardiff, Carmarthenshire, Anglesey, Denbighshire, Flintshire, Wrexham, Powys, Pembrokeshire, Swansea and Vale of Glamorgan councils are among those now building their own homes again. (126)

TV property show presenter George Clarke gives support for council housing

George Clarke, architect and presenter of property shows on Channel television, launched a campaign for the Government to build 100,000 council houses every year. His petition reached over 60,000 within 24 hours of it being opened. (133)

Southwark. One year on from bringing all of Southwark's responsive housing repairs in house the council has declared its DLO a success and its support for the future. (130)

Sources

(1)   South London Press picture and article, Lump labour protest 1974

(2)   Building Workers' Strike of 1972, Workers Power website, 2017

(3)   175 years of Building Trades Unionism, UCATT publication 2002

(4)   Building Workers' Strike 1972 History, UCATT website, July 2017

(5)   Outside Mile End site against TOB victimisation 1973, Workers Press

(6)   Shrewsbury Wigan to London March, Workers Press December 1974

(7)   Protest outside TUC over the Shrewsbury 24, Report Digital 1974

(8)   UCATT (now UNITE) umbrella companies website 6th August 2018

(9)   Motion by UCATT to TUC umbrella companies. Website 7/09/2014

(10)   Southwark Council's public services committee items, September 1982

(11)   Daily Mail article, December 2006

(12)   Full list of OFT bid-rigging fines, Guardian 22/09/2009 & OFT web

(13)   hansard.parliament.uk/commons/1952-11-07/debates/9a8f004b-3540-4b1b-874d-cdd99c0bfd1c/LondonBuildersConference

(14)   The Builders' Conference, website 2017

(15)   Early Direct Labour Organisations, Labour Monthly, November 1920

(16)   "Building with Direct Labour", pamphlet, Direct Labour Collective, 1978

(17)   Labour Research Department book on direct labour, 1928

(18)   Livesey Museum, 1930s, Bermondsey DLO

(19)   Westminster, The Build Environment, Workshop, 13th July 2017

(20)   Local Authority Building & Allied Trades Agreement

(21)   Bovis, compensation, badly built homes. Guardian website 20/02/2017

(22)   Extract from 'Blowout', The paper of the oil workers' trade union

(23)   Construction loss of 175,000 EU workers, Guardian, 15 May 2017

(24)   Dir. Christine Wall, Tradeswomen and DLOs, seminar, 13 July 2016

(25)   The Consultancy Association

(26)   Braganza St dispute, JCC BW, 19 February 1980

(27)   Transfer of the GLC and ILEA building workers to Southwark

(28)   Housing Action Trust, Hansard; & Southwark DLO postcard

Sources

(29) Working Rule Agreement, private sector, Building Industry 1970-1980

(30) New build DLO Organisation, "Southwark Construction" pamphlet

(31) Defend Council Housing, John Grayson, housing bulletin 2006

(32) Advert for (CABIN), to oppose direct labour 1978

(33) 1976, Southwark Letter, housing committee councillor Charles Sawyer.

(34) Interserve collapse, Guardian 18th March 2019

(35) Land now 52% of UK net worth, Guardian website 29/9/2018

(36) UCATT letter to stewards banning use of asbestos

(37) J Kennedy report to UCATT Regional Council 1979

(38) Chargehands' contracts. Southwark establishment ctte 19/02/1980

(39) Actions in support of the 1984-85 Miners' Strike

(40) Painters' strike, Arnolds estate April 1980

(41) Arnold estate strike over sacking of stores labourer 1980

(42) South London Press article on 1991 jobs strike

(43) Letter to Tony Ritchie, Southwark council leader 21 March 1986

(44) Evening Standard picture and article 1976

(45) Herald Express 2017

(46) TUC website article 2016

(47) The Housing And Planning Act 2016

(50) Billions in underwriting guarantees, National Housing Federation

(51) Richard Laco death, court findings, 21 April 2017 news info

(52) Construction Enquirer, construction fines highest levels 9 May 2017

(53) Asbestos convention, Hazards, 3 May 2017

(54) Dave Smith blacklisting, Morning Star 3 May 2017

(55) Construction company fined £750,000, 4 May 2017

(56) Asbestos exports by companies registered in UK, CSC 12 May 2017

(57) Housing benefit bill £25bn, BBC website Sept 2015

(58) Support for mortgage interest payments, UK gov website

(59) Renovation grants, Citizens Advice website

(60) Private residence capital gain tax relief. UK.gov website.

Sources

(61) 2.5mhomes sold under right-to-buy, Evening Standard website January 18th 2009.

(62) Construction manager jailed 4 years, Crown Prosecution 30 June 2017

(63) The rise in housing costs, Open Democracy website

(64) UNITE reveals bogus-self-employment, press release 31 July 2017

(65) Southwark Council report: investing in council housing, Options 2012

(66) Blacklisting 10 years on, Phil Chamberlain, March 6, 2019

(67) 24,000 council homes built before 1914, J Boughton, Municipal Dreams

(68) Wilson Grove estate, Southwark Local History Library/Archive

(69) Guardian newspaper, Delay of Grenfell inquiry.2/05/2019

(70) Independent: Delay in criminal charges at Grenfell, March 2019

(71) Southwark Council regenerations, 35% Campaign website

(72) Southwark, private housing company, Southwark News, 30th July 2015

(73) Zero-hour contracts in London, ONLONDON website

(74) Cuts to the Employment Support Allowance, gov.uk website

(75) London low paid in 2018, Trust for London website

(76) Public and private sector tenants' rents, Tenants Voice website

(77) The Housing & Planning Act 2016, UNISON briefing paper 2016

(78) A third of tenants moved to outside London, BBC news online Sep 2015

(79) All that is Solid – Danny Dorling 2015

(80) English Heritage, Teachers Notes: brief history of social (council) housing, Website

(81) Housing benefit cap.gov.uk/benefit-cap

(82) Leeds Tenants Federation history, website May 2017

(83) 2008 University of the West of England, Bristol, Website

(84) Socialist Party Magazine, Website

(85) A Social History of Housing 1815 - 1985. (by John Burnett 1986)

(86) The Leeds rent strike in 1914; by Quintin Bradley, website 2017

Sources

(87)   Red Clydeside: history in Glasgow 1910-1932, website May 2017

(88)   The Rent Strike 1915 and "Mrs Mary Barbour's Army", Website

(89)   Living Heritage, Website 2017

(90)   The 1988 Housing Act' introduced "Tenants Choice" Legislation, gov.uk

(91)   Government increases right-to-buy discount, HM Government website

(92)   Rent Strikes: Direct Action, Socialist Register website 2017

(93)   Corruption of Poulson and T Dan Smith, The Journal website March 2004

(94)   Blair/Brown governments build 7,870 homes, Full Fact website 2013

(95)   The Beveridge Report, Guardian newspaper 29th March 2017

(96)   The 1996 Housing Act; Housing Review website

(97)   Conservatives increased Right-to-Buy, discount, The Independent Feb 2018

(98)   The Struggle against the Housing Finance Act, by Leslie Sklair

(99)   Shelter centenary online publication

(100)   DCLG Statistics, Table 104, Live Tables on Housing Stock

(101)   ALMOs July 2017, Wikimedia website 2017

(102)   In 1979, 42% of Britons lived in council homes, Guardian Jan 2016

(103)   The 1965 Rent Act, Hansard website 1966

(104)   Ken Loach's film "Cathy Come Home", YouTube panel discussion 2016

(105)   This is Money online, April 2016 (Housing cost report)

(106)   Rogue landlords break the law, Guardian online 15th April 2019

(107)   Web Housing Statistical Release, 24 May 2018

(108)   Old Kent Road redevelopment, South London Press 5/04/2019

(109)   Land Hoarding, 19th April 2019 (Private Eye and Guardian online)

(110)   Vacant dwellings in England, Housing Statistical Release 24/05/2018

(111)   The 1944 Dudley report into housing, The Spectator

(112)   Labour in 1964 aimed to build 500,000 homes, wikipedia.org

(113)   Parker Morris Report, English Heritage website.

(114)   Introducing the London Living Rent, Guardian 3rd November 2016

(115)   Ledbury estate's tower blocks, Southwark News Oct 2018

(116)   Affordable rent study, Southwark Council 2015

(117)   Aylesbury estate, Guardian 12th September 2018

(118)   No-fought evictions announcement, BBC website 15th April 2019

(119)   Pensioners and Housing, NPC election manifesto 2017

(120)   Housing Acts of 1985 and 1988, Guardian March 18th, 2017

(121)   BBC Radio 4, May 2015 on affordable housing

(122)   May 2016, Guardian. Spending over50% of income on housing.

(123)   Privatisation threats to Haringey Homes; Paul Burnham HDCH 2019

(124)   Growing movement to bring back DLOs, Guardian 29/05/2019

(125)   Linda Clark. Presentation at Brussels on UK DLOs, 20/06/2019

(126)   Wales building new council homes, BBC online 29/04/2019

(127)   Liverpool council build new homes, BBC online 21/06/2019

(128)   Lowest on record 30 construction deaths in 2018/2019, HSE

(129)   MPs report 2m older people are suffering, Guardian 4/07/2019

(130)   Southwark council declared its DLO a success

(132)   Rich households benefit from £25bn public subsidy, Guardian 31/08/2019

(133)   TV property show presenter George Clarke support for council housing, C4 August 2019

(134)   Nearly 2 years since Carillion collapse. UNITE 2/09/2019 Web.

Index

Arm's Length Management Organizations 226,

Apprentices, 11-12, 14- 15, 18, 60, 68-69, 70-71, 81, 83, 90,115, 119, 135,138-139,153,230.

Amalgamated Society of Woodworkers, 12, 19, 22,25.

Asbestos, 19-21, 48-49, 69, 79, 84, 93, 119-120, 144-148, 155-156, 158, 164-166, 168, 171-172, 176-177.

Aylesbury estate, 18, 23, 31, 49. 201-206-207.

Amalgamated Society of Painters and Decorators, 25.

Amalgamated Society of Building Trades Workers, 25.

Arnolds estate, 99.

Direct Labour Organisations, 11,13, 15, 39,53, 68, 95, 145, 172, 174, 228.

Blacklisting, 11, 24, 26, 29, 68-69 73, 125, 129, 165, 167, 178, 205.

Bermondsey council. 56, 73, 201.

Bovis, 21, 48, 68, 73, 81

Battersea, 54, 157.

Bonus Schemes, 34, 57, 66, 83, 88.

Botes, 123-125, 128, 172.

Construction Safety Campaign, 12, 84, 110, 142-143, 148, 151-152, 155, 162, 164. 166

Camden estate, 59, 93.

Contract rigging and price fixing, 39, 47, 62, 69, 122, 173, 220.

Consultancy association, 73.

Camden DLO, 59, 90, 102.

CABIN, 64, 95.

Copland Road depot, 80-82, 93, 104, 109-110.

Cranes, 48, 157, 160.

Dave Smith, 165-167.

Defend Council Housing, 84, 193-194, 201.

Eric Heffer, 95, 149.

Environment, 13, 47,73, 120, 126, 148, 175, 177, 182, 228.

EEPTU, 83, 108, 115, 136.

EPIU, 136.

Frensham St depot, 81, 115, 124-125.

Fred Stansbury, 19, 76, 136.

Fernett, 112, 115-116.

Fines, 40-41, 45, 150, 158,164.

236

Index

Index

Opti-time, 131.

Oil based paint, 141-142.

Progressives, 53-54.

Pensions, 11, 36-37, 88, 100, 135, 140-141, 144, 159, 169.

Poll tax, 86, 104, 109-110, 193, 211.

Redundancy, 31, 34, 79, 91, 100, 111, 119, 124, 134-135.

Rate capping, 84, 104-105, 107.

Relatives support group, 154.

Rents, 68, 184-193, 195-197, 205-206, 208, 210, 213-215, 217, 220-223, 228-229.

Sacking, 22, 24, 30, 98.

Stewards, 15, 25-26, 29-30, 76, 83-86, 89, 91, 93, 96-97, 99, 114-116, 118-119, 124, 129, 135-139, 141, 146, 150, 153, 171.

Southwark Council, 12-15, 18, 21, 23, 33, 40, 42, 47-50, 67, 73-74, 77, 81, 86, 105, 107, 111, 120, 123-124, 128-129, 134-135, 137, 145, 148, 171-172, 180, 182, 202, 204-206-208.

Self-employment, 25, 33, 35-38, 178.

Shrewsbury Building Workers, 27, 29, 31-32, 68, 84.

Southwark Construction, 63, 73, 79, 83, 97-98, 138.

Spa Road depot, 76, 78, 80-81, 93-94, 200.

Strikes, 23,26, 33, 100, 102,106, 185-187, 191, 211.

Southwark DLO, 19, 40, 67, 71, 73, 79-80, 88, 98, 100, 104, 106, 123, 125, 140, 145, 147-150, 156, 163.

The Right to Buy, 14, 192, 197, 199, 209.

Transport and General Workers' Union, 25.

Trollope and Colls, 24-25, 50-51.

Training, 11, 15, 19, 34, 50, 60, 68, 70-71, 138, 171, 176-177.

TUPE, 79, 84, 107, 118, 123-125, 128, 175.

Tenants, 11, 15, 50, 65, 67-69, 80, 84, 86, 88, 90, 105, 119-120, 129, 160, 171-172, 175, 182,184-187, 189-197, 200, 202, 205-206, 209-2011, 215-216, 218, 223, 228-229.

Tenant Management Organisations 171, 211, 229.

Tony Ritchie, 105, 107.

Tripp, 118, 123-124.

Umbrella Companies, 11, 35-38, 174, 178.

Index

Other extra copies of this book as well as other publications by the author Tony O' Brien. For enquires phone 07500169151

THE FIGHT TO BAN ASBESTOS
1995 - 2000

CONSTRUCTION SAFETY
CAMPAIGN

By Tony O' Brien

CONSTRUCTION
SAFETY CAMPAIGN
Over 20 years fighting for workers'
health and safety

Tony O'Brien

Price £3   Price £10

"Tackling the Housing Crisis". book priced £10 plus £2 postage. Payments made to: "Tony O' Brien". For enquiries phone 07500169151

HOW TO GET ADVANCED ORDERS OF THE BOOK EITHER:

Complete the form and address it together with a cheque to: 'Tony O' Brien' c/o Southwark Pensioners Centre, 307 Camberwell Rd, Camberwell, London SE5 0HQ.

OR complete the form & send to: tonysalebook@outlook.com. Send amount by transfer to HSBC bank account number: 01773496. Sort code: 400525

<u>Please fill in your details below:</u>

NAME...

ADDRESS..

EMAIL...

PHONE..

Number of books required: ....

Total cost including postage..............